Third Edit.

The Technical
COMMUNICATIONS
COMPANION

A Reference Guide & Workbook

Ron Rogers | Melanie Parrish
LUZERNE COUNTY COMMUNITY COLLEGE

Kendall Hunt
publishing company

www.kendallhunt.com
Send all inquiries to:
4050 Westmark Drive
Dubuque, IA 52004-1840

ISBN 978-1-5249-7164-9

Published in the United States of America

TABLE OF CONTENTS

Chapter 1   Audience and Purpose   1

Chapter 2   Ethics and the Workplace   9

Chapter 3   Correspondence   23

Chapter 4   Document Design and Graphics   43

Chapter 5   Presentations   63

Chapter 6   Instructions   71

Chapter 7   Employment Communication   81

Chapter 8   Technical Research   123

Chapter 9   Proposals   137

Chapter 10   Recommendations   149

Chapter 11   Writing for the Web   161

CHAPTER 1

Audience and Purpose

Organization of Ideas in Technical Documents.

Within technical documents of all types, a certain pattern of organization occurs, providing a consistent location for various ideas. Technical communication ALWAYS considers the **audience** of any document and with this consideration in mind, the reader will be able to locate various pieces of information in a standard location, regardless of the type of document created. All documents, technical or not, follow the pattern of **introduction**, **body** and **conclusion**. Technical writing will strive to achieve certain objectives within the three areas that may differ from other types of writing that you may have experienced.

Introduction

All documents need to have an introduction that will inform the reader of various things. Within this section, the topic will be introduced. The reader will not have a background for any type of document that you are presenting and you must provide it. What is this document about? How can the reader use this information? Both of these questions need to be answered in the Introduction of a document. Also with the introduction should be some type of thesis statement that indicates what the main ideas are to be included. The reader will be able to find more information about each of the ideas as he/she continues to read the document.

Body

This is the main section of any document, be it one paragraph in a memo or several pages within a proposal. This area will provide any details the reader needs to know, may not already know and will need for more understanding of the subject matter. As mentioned, this section may be relatively short, as in one paragraph, or may take several pages of writing to complete, as in a proposal. There is no length maximum here. You will need to include whatever information is needed for the reader to clearly understand the topic.

Body paragraphs have, as a goal, the objective to provide details of the subject matter. You may create paragraphs that explain why something has happened as it did. You may be providing reasons why someone should accept your argument for an action to take place. You may be providing research that is needed to understand what steps need to be taken next. A simple description of steps can be included in the body. Commonly, you may include statistical information here as well. Specifications of a product or a service can be found in body paragraphs. Here is where you need to include the pieces of information, with explanation for the readers. At no point should the reader be asking "Why did this happen?" or "What do I need to know?" after reading your body paragraphs.

Frequently, body paragraphs will also contain graphics to help illustrate what is being communicated in word form. It is quite common to see an illustration of an idea included with the paragraph. This is done for reader clarity and retention. Body paragraphs may also present information in lists rather than typical sentence structure within a paragraph. Listing is a great way to relate several items pertaining to one subject matter and do so in a very concise format.

Conclusion

This section is very important in any document and technical writing is no exception. It is similar to other types of writing by including a summary of information presented in the document. It is different in that any action that needs to be taken by the reader must be specified in this section. If you are requesting a meeting, for example from your supervisor, that should be stated in the Conclusion of the document. As the writer, you need to consider what action you want completed, who needs to do the action and when the action needs to be completed. It is very important that these ideas are communicated clearly. If you include any references or vague statements, you have very little chance of the action needed being completed by the reader. It is always a great idea to include a form of communication within the conclusion. This may be as simple as including an email address or a phone number and extension for the person responsible for the content. This person may or may not be the writer of the document. This may help make the action easier to accomplish. This will also indicate that you, or the appropriate person for this topic, is approachable for further information.

As you can see, the basic organization can apply to any length of document or any type of document that you will need to create within a technical writing realm. Regardless of the type of document, you will be creating three paragraphs or three sections in order to accommodate these objectives within an Introduction, Body and Conclusion.

Excerpt from a Document for Experts

The writer uses technical terms and does not define or explain them.

Zoonotic filarial infestations occur worldwide, and in most reported cases the involved species are members of the genus *Dirofilaria*. However, zoonotic *Onchocerca* infections are rare and to date only 13 cases (originating from Europe, Russia, the United States, Canada, and Japan) have been described. In all of these cases only 1 immature worm was found, and the causative species was identified as *O. gutturosa, O. cervicalis, O. reticulata,* or *O. dewittei japonica* on the basis of morphologic and in some cases serologic parameters *(1–4). O. cervicalis* and *O. reticulata* are found in the ligaments of the neck and extremities of horses, *O. gutturosa* is typically found in the nuchal ligaments of cattle, and *O. dewittei japonica* is found in the distal parts of the limbs and adipose tissue of footpads of wild boars.

The writer presents information directly.

We identified the causative agent of a zoonotic *Onchocerca* infection with multiple nodules in a patient with systemic lupus erythematosus (SLE) who had been receiving hemodialysis. The parasite was identified in paraffin-embedded tissue samples by PCR and DNA sequence analysis.

The Study

The writer uses abbreviations the readers will understand.

The patient was a 59-year-old woman with SLE who had developed multiple nodules on the neck and face over several years. Because of major renal insufficiency, she also had been receiving hemodialysis 3 times per week (3.5 hours) for >10 years. The first clinical differential diagnoses were cutaneous SLE,

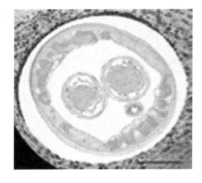

nephrogenous dermatopathy, calciphylaxis, and calcinosis. The clinical picture was obscured by secondary inflammations and ulcerations caused by self-inflicted trauma. Multiple sampling attempts by cutaneous core biopsies resulted in histologic diagnosis of unspecific, secondary inflammatory changes. Deep surgical excision of 1 subcutaneous nodule on the scalp indicated subcutaneous helminthosis. The patient was treated with ivermectin and subjected to 2 plastic surgeries for facial reconstruction, after which she recovered.

Source: Koehsler, M., et al. (2007). Reprinted from *Onchocerca jakutensis* filariasis in humans. *Emerging Infectious Diseases Journal,* 13(11), 1749-52.

Document for Technicians with High-Level Expertise

Bench Aids for the diagnosis of filarial infections   **Introduction**

World Health Organization 1997

Introduction

Several species of filarial worms infect humans in the tropical and subtropical regions of the world. The adult worms inhabit various tissues and organs of the body and are inaccessible for identification. Consequently, diagnosis of filarial infections depends primarily on the identification of the larval stage of the parasite (microfilaria). Most species of microfilaria circulate in peripheral blood; however, some are found in the skin.

The microfilaria

The writers include practical information to help technicians identify microfilaria.

At the light-microscopic level and with the aid of a variety of stains, a microfilaria appears as a primitive organism, serpentine in shape and filled with the nuclei of many cells. In many, but not all, species, the body may be enveloped in a membrane called a sheath (**sh**). Where a sheath is present it may extend a short or long distance beyond either extremity of the microfilaria. In some species, depending on the stain used, the sheath displays a characteristic staining quality which aids in species identification. The nuclei of the cells that fill the body are usually darkly stained and may be crowded together or dispersed. The anterior extremity is typically devoid of nuclei and is called the cephalic or head space (**hs**); it may be short or long. Along the body of the microfilaria there are additional spaces and cells that serve as anatomical landmarks. These include the nerve ring (**nr**), excretory pore (**ep**), excretory cell (**ec**), and anal port (**ap**). In some species, an amorphous mass called the innerbody (**ib**) and four small cells called the rectal cells (**R-1, R-2, R-3, R-4**) can be seen, usually with the aid of special stains. These structures and their positions are sometimes useful for species identification. The shape of the tail and the presence or absence and distribution of nuclei within it are also important in species identification.

Periodicity

The writers use technical terminology, yet define some terms and concepts technicians will not understand.

Some species of microfilariae circulate in peripheral blood at all hours of the day and night, while others are present only during certain periods. The fluctuation in numbers of microfilariae present in peripheral blood during a 24-hour period is referred to as periodicity. Species that are found in the blood during night-time hours but are absent at other times are designated **nocturnally periodic** (e.g. **Wuchereria bancrofti, Brugia malayi**); those that are present only during certain daytime hours are designated **diurnally periodic** (e.g. **Loa loa**). Microfilariae that are normally present in the blood at all hours but whose density increases significantly during either the night or the day are referred to as **subperiodic**. Microfilariae that circulate in the blood throughout a 24-hour period without significant changes in their numbers are referred to as **nonperiodic** or **aperiodic** (e.g. **Mansonella** spp.).

The periodicity of a given species or geographical variant is especially useful in determining the best time of day to collect blood samples for examination. To determine microfilarial periodicity in an individual, it is necessary to examine measured quantities of peripheral blood collected at consecutive intervals of 2 or 4 hours over a period of 24–30 hours.

Procedures for Technicians with Mid-Level Expertise

Specimen Processing

Preparing Blood Smears

If you are using venous blood, blood smears should be prepared as soon as possible after collection (delay can result in changes in parasite morphology and staining characteristics).

Thick smears

Thick smears consist of a thick layer of dehemoglobinized (lysed) red blood cells (RBCs). The blood elements (including parasites, if any) are more concentrated than in an equal area of a thin smear. Thus, thick smears allow a more efficient detection of parasites (increased sensitivity). However, they do not permit an optimal review of parasite morphology. For example, they are often not adequate for species identification of malaria parasites: if the thick smear is positive for malaria parasites, the thin smear should be used for species identification.

The writers include procedural information. → Prepare at least 2 smears per patient!

1. Place a small drop of blood in the center of the pre-cleaned, labeled slide.
2. Using the corner of another slide or an applicator stick, spread the drop in a circular pattern until it is the size of a dime (1.5 cm^2).
3. A thick smear of proper density is one which, if placed (wet) over newsprint, allows you to barely read the words.
4. Lay the slides flat and allow the smears to dry thoroughly (protect from dust and insects!). Insufficiently dried smears (and/or smears that are too thick) can detach from the slides during staining. The risk is increased in smears made with anticoagulated blood. At room temperature, drying can take several hours; 30 minutes is the minimum; in the latter case, handle the smear very delicately during staining. You can accelerate the drying by using a fan or hair dryer (use cool setting). Protect thick smears from hot environments to prevent heat-fixing the smear.
5. Do not fix thick smears with methanol or heat. If there will be a delay in staining smears, dip the thick smear briefly in water to hemolyse the RBCs.

From *Technical Communication* by Brenda Sims. Copyright © 2015 by Kendall Hunt Publishing Company. Reprinted by permission.

Document for Managers

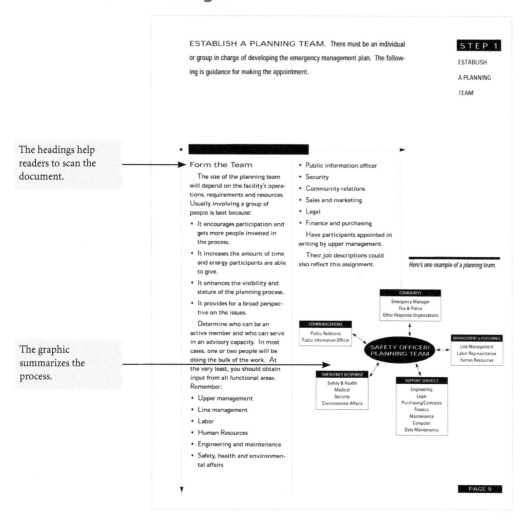

ESTABLISH A PLANNING TEAM. There must be an individual or group in charge of developing the emergency management plan. The following is guidance for making the appointment.

STEP 1
ESTABLISH
A PLANNING
TEAM

The headings help readers to scan the document.

Form the Team

The size of the planning team will depend on the facility's operations, requirements and resources. Usually involving a group of people is best because:

- It encourages participation and gets more people invested in the process.
- It increases the amount of time and energy participants are able to give.
- It enhances the visibility and stature of the planning process.
- It provides for a broad perspective on the issues.

Determine who can be an active member and who can serve in an advisory capacity. In most cases, one or two people will be doing the bulk of the work. At the very least, you should obtain input from all functional areas. Remember:

- Upper management
- Line management
- Labor
- Human Resources
- Engineering and maintenance
- Safety, health and environmental affairs

- Public information officer
- Security
- Community relations
- Sales and marketing
- Legal
- Finance and purchasing

Have participants appointed in writing by upper management.

Their job descriptions could also reflect this assignment.

Here's one example of a planning team.

COMMUNITY
Emergency Manager
Fire & Police
Other Response Organizations

COMMUNICATIONS
Public Relations
Public Information Officer

SAFETY OFFICER/
PLANNING TEAM

MANAGEMENT & PERSONNEL
Line Management
Labor Representative
Human Resources

EMERGENCY RESPONSE
Safety & Health
Medical
Security
Environmental Affairs

SUPPORT SERVICES
Engineering
Legal
Purchasing/Contracts
Finance
Maintenance
Computer
Data Maintenance

PAGE 9

The graphic summarizes the process.

Source: Federal Emergency Management Agency. (1993, October 1). *Emergency Management Guide for Business and Industry*. Retrieved from www.fema.gov/pdf/library/bizindst.pdf.

From *Technical Communication* by Brenda Sims. Copyright © 2015 by Kendall Hunt Publishing Company. Reprinted by permission.

Document for General Readers

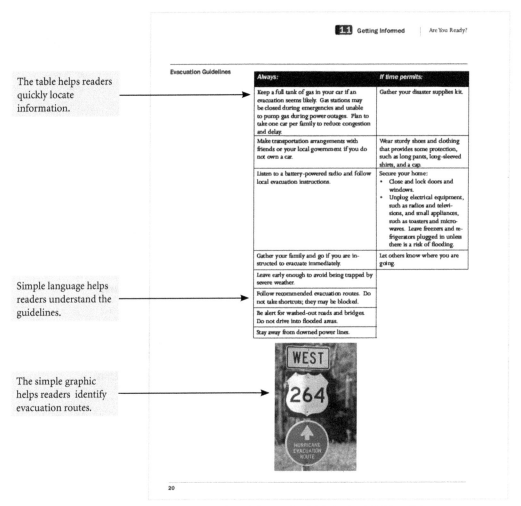

The table helps readers quickly locate information.

Simple language helps readers understand the guidelines.

The simple graphic helps readers identify evacuation routes.

Source: Federal Emergency Management Agency. (2004). *Are you Ready? An In-depth Guide to Citizen Preparedness.* Retrieved from www.fema.gov/pdf/library/bizindst.pdf. FEMA, *Are You Ready?*
From *Technical Writing in the Workplace* by Harvey Ussach. Copyright © 2014 by Kendall Hunt Publishing Company. Reprinted by permission.

Communication Purpose Worksheet

The purpose of this (document type) _____

Is to (writer's purpose) _____

So that (reader's purpose) _____

From *Technical Writing in the Workplace* by Harvey Ussach. Copyright © 2014 by Kendall Hunt Publishing Company. Reprinted by permission.

CHAPTER 2

Ethics and the Workplace

Each one of us has a "code" that we rely on to guide our behaviors on a personal level. These codes tell us how we should behave or what should be said in certain situations. We gain our ethics from various aspects of our lives, some having stronger influences than others on each of us. Businesses and professions are no different. The employees of a business or a profession are expected to act and speak in a certain way in the workplace. Each of these areas creates a code of ethics or a code of behavior for all levels of employees to follow. As you enter a career field or business, you need to be aware of what is expected of you in the workplace. You need to find and understand the code of ethics for that business or career.

Proctor & Gamble's Business Code of Conduct

At the core of P&G is the commitment to doing the right thing. This commitment has been passed down from generation to generation of P&Gers. If you are ever unsure about a business action or decision, you should ask yourself the following questions:

- Am I being truthful and honest?
- Is it "the right thing" to do?
- Would I feel comfortable if it was reported in the news or to someone I respect?
- Will it protect P&G's reputation?

If the answer to any of these questions is "no," or you are not sure, do not proceed. Always ask before acting.

Source: Proctor & Gamble. (2010). *P&G: Our worldwide business conduct manual: We do the right thing.* (p. 5). Retrieved from http://www.pg.com/en_US/downloads/company/governance/Policy_Worldwide_Business_Conduct_Manual.pdf.

From *Technical Communication* by Brenda Sims. Copyright © 2015 by Kendall Hunt Publishing Company. Reprinted by permission.

Kraft Foods Guide to Ethical Dilemmas

Integrity: Doing What Is Right

Ask Before Acting

- Is it legal?
- Does it follow company policy?
- Is it right?
- How would it look to those outside the company? For example, how would it look to our customers, the people in the communities where we work, and the general public?

Remember These Rules

- Know the legal and company standards that apply to your job.
- Follow these standards—always.
- Ask if you are ever unsure what's the right thing to do.
- Keep asking until you get the answer.

Kraft Foods is the world's largest manufacturer and marketer of consumer packaged goods.

Source: Kraft Foods. (2009, March). Our way of doing business: The Kraft Foods code of conduct. Retrieved from http://www.kraft.com/assets/pdf/KraftFoods_CodeofConduct.pdf.

From *Technical Communication* by Brenda Sims. Copyright © 2015 by Kendall Hunt Publishing Company. Reprinted by permission.

Technical writers must follow some ethical considerations in creating various documents within the workplace. One well-noted aspect of writing is to cite sources used within documents so as not to plagiarize someone's ideas. This is not something unique to a classroom setting. This happens in the workplace also. Sources need to be cited according to an appropriate method for the field.

What Is Fair Use?

The U.S. Copyright website explains that the law sets out four factors to consider when determining fair use:

- **The purpose and character of the use, including whether such use is of a commercial nature or is for nonprofit educational purposes.** For example, fair use guidelines are applied more liberally to schools and more conservatively to for-profit organizations.
- **The nature of the copyrighted work.** If the work is essential to the public, fair use guidelines are applied more liberally than if the work is non-essential to the public.
- **The amount and substantiality of the portion used in relation to the copyrighted work as a whole.** For example, 2 pages of a 100-page document are a small portion, while 2 pages of a 4-page document are a large portion. The law does not specify a specific amount or percentage that you may use without written permission.
- **The effect of the use on the potential market for or value of the copyrighted work.** If the use of the copyrighted material would hurt the owner's potential for profit, then you have probably violated fair use guidelines.

Source: U. S. Copyright Office (2015). More information on fair use. Retrieved June 8, 2015, from http://copyright.gov/fair-use/more-info.html

TIPS for Following Copyright Laws

- **Follow fair use guidelines.** Do not rely on excessive amounts of material borrowed from other sources unless that information is repurposed from your company. Fair use guidelines do not apply to graphics, so you must always seek written permission to use a graphic.
- **When in doubt about fair use, obtain written permission.** The fair use guidelines can be confusing because the law does not provide a specific number of words, lines, or notes that you may legally use without permission. If you are unsure whether you are following fair use guidelines, ask for permission to use the material. If you cannot gain permission, do not use the copyrighted material.
- **Cite the source of material that does not belong to you or your organization.** The U.S. Copyright Office notes that simply acknowledging the source of the copyrighted material does not substitute for obtaining permission. By citing your sources, you also fulfill your ethical responsibility to be honest.
- **Ask for guidance from legal counsel.** If you need help understanding copyright laws, ask your organization's legal counsel for help. Don't guess or assume that you are following the law correctly.

From *Technical Communication* by Brenda Sims. Copyright © 2015 by Kendall Hunt Publishing Company. Reprinted by permission.

TIPS for Protecting a Trademark

- **Use the trademark or registered trademark symbol.** Each time you include the name of a trademarked product, use the appropriate symbol. If you are unsure whether a product is trademarked, go to the website for the U.S. Office of Patent and Trademarks, www.uspto.gov.
- **Use a footnote the first time you use a trademark.** At least once in a document, preferably near the beginning, follow the trademark or registered trademark symbol with an asterisk or footnote number. In the footnote, state that the product is a trademark or registered trademark. For example, a footnote might read: [1]Kleenex is a registered trademark of Kimberly-Clark Corporation.
- **Use the trademark as an adjective, not as a noun.** For example, you would write: Doritos® tortilla chips, not simply Doritos®. Likewise, you would write: Dr. Pepper™ soft drink, not Dr. Pepper™.
- **Don't do anything to hurt the spirit of the trademark or to alter the trademark.** Do not change the trademark in any way. For example, if the trademark uses a particular color or font, do not change that color or font.

From *Technical Communication* by Brenda Sims. Copyright © 2015 by Kendall Hunt Publishing Company. Reprinted by permission.

TIPS for Following Liability Laws

You can protect your organization and yourself from possible liability suits by following these tips adapted from Pamela S. Helyar, (1992), author of *Product Liability: Meeting Legal Standards for Adequate Instructions.*

- **Use language and graphics that the users will understand.** For example, if you are writing a manual that children will use, include simple, clear graphics that children can easily follow. If you are writing a manual for nonnative speakers of English, use simple language free of ***idioms*** (expressions whose meanings are different from the standard or literal meanings of the words they contain: e.g., going cold turkey).

- **Tell the user how the product works and what it can and cannot do.** Make sure that your users understand what the product does. You can be liable if you do not also explain what the product cannot do.

- **Warn the users of risks when using the product.** State the specific dangers in using the product. Use direct, clear language. Don't assume that readers will know the danger. You are responsible for directly stating that danger.

- **Make sure that users can easily see the warnings.** For example, if you are warning users of the risk of cutting their fingers or toes with a lawn mower, put the warning both in the instruction manual and on the mower.

- **Tell users what the product can do and what it can't or shouldn't do.** Tell users what the product is designed to do and what it isn't designed to do. Put this information not only in the instruction manual that will accompany the product, but also in materials that a potential buyer will see. For example, a manual for a gas barbecue grill states: "For outdoor use only. Never operate grill in enclosed areas, as an explosion or a carbon monoxide buildup might occur, which could result in injury or death" (Coleman, 1999). While most users would know that they should operate a barbecue grill only outside, the manufacturer could be liable if it didn't warn users of the risk of using the grill indoors.

- **Inform users of all aspects of owning the product, from maintaining to disposing of the product.** When purchasing some products or services, the user may have ongoing responsibilities; you must inform the user of these responsibilities. For example, most car manuals provide owners with a maintenance schedule. Along with the schedule, the manual usually includes a statement such as "If your vehicle is damaged because you failed to follow the recommended maintenance schedule and/or to use or maintain fluids, fuel, lubricants, or refrigerants recommended in this manual, your warranty may be invalid and may not cover the damage."

- **Test the product and the accompanying product information.** Perform usability testing to make sure the product is safe and that the instructions and product information are accurate. For information on usability testing, see Chapter 18.

From *Technical Communication* by Brenda Sims. Copyright © 2015 by Kendall Hunt Publishing Company. Reprinted by permission.

TIPS for Making Ethical Decisions

- **Gather all related information.** Make sure you have all the facts and that your facts are accurate. You don't want to risk losing your job or your reputation by basing a decision on inaccurate or incomplete information.
- **Think first; then act.** Once you are satisfied you have all the facts and they are accurate, think about all the possible choices and use the questions in the section, Ask the Right Questions. Once you are satisfied you have made the ethical choice, take action or communicate your decision.
- **Find out all you can about the people affected by your decision and those who will read your communication.** You can then determine the best way to approach these people if you want to argue for change or you need to suggest a course of action that they may not want to consider.
- **Talk to people whom you trust.** They may help you consider alternative, yet ethical choices. If you feel you cannot trust anyone in your organization, talk to someone whom you trust outside the organization. Don't face the situation alone.
- **Aim to establish a reputation as a hardworking, loyal coworker with integrity.** Then, when you do take a stand on an ethical issue, your coworkers and managers will take your stand seriously.

From *Technical Communication* by Brenda Sims. Copyright © 2015 by Kendall Hunt Publishing Company. Reprinted by permission.

Taking it to the Workplace

Understanding Ethics in Your Profession

Many professional organizations have developed a code of conduct or a code of ethics for their members. These codes give members standards for ethical behavior in their profession. While these codes are hard to enforce, they do guide the organization's members in ethical professional behavior. Many companies have also adopted codes of conduct or ethics. These codes give members guidelines for ethical behavior and inform the public about how its members and employees will conduct business.

Assignment

Assume that you are a recent college graduate and have started a new job. You plan to join a professional organization in your field.

1. Find a professional organization in your field.
2. Find out if the organization has a code of ethics. (If not, find another organization related to your field.) Most professional organizations post their code of ethics on their website.
3. Bring a copy of the code of ethics to class.
4. Be prepared to answer these questions about the code:
   - Does the code provide a model for making ethical decisions?
   - How effectively does the code protect the interests of the public? Of the professional organization? What specific words or phrases demonstrate this effectiveness?
   - How can the professional organization enforce the code?
   - Does the code help the members make ethical decisions? If so, how? If not, what would you include in the code?

iStockphoto.com 2008

Case Study Analysis

The Human Radiation Experiments

Background

From the 1940s to the 1970s, patients, some terminally ill, were injected with plutonium—mostly without their knowledge or consent—at Oak Ridge Hospital, the University of Rochester, the University of Chicago, and the University of California. In the years following the atomic bombings of the Japanese cities Hiroshima and Nagasaki, the U.S. military and nuclear weapons industry wanted data on the biological effects of plutonium and radioisotopes. To determine these effects, Manhattan Project scientists injected 18 unsuspecting patients with plutonium. All these patients had already been diagnosed with terminal diseases and weren't expected to live more than 10 years. Some of the patients, according to investigators at the Atomic Energy Commission, had not granted informed consent. The patients who had granted consent did so under false pretenses because the word plutonium was classified during World War II. Those patients who survived did not even know that they had been injected with plutonium until 1974.

These experiments continued during the Cold War, when the U.S. military wanted to know how much radiation a soldier could endure before becoming disabled even though researchers were aware of the hazards of working with plutonium as early as January 5, 1944. From 1960 to 1971, scientists at the University of Cincinnati performed experiments on 88 cancer patients ranging in age from 9 to 84. These patients were repeatedly exposed to massive doses of radiation, yet medical researchers from the 1930s through the 1950s had determined that whole-body radiation was ineffective in treating most cancers. These patients had tumors that would resist radiation—a fact that the doctors already knew (Braffman-Miller, 1995). Most of these patients were uneducated, had low IQs, and were poor. The researchers in charge of these experiments wrote in 1969 that "directional radiation will be attempted since this type of exposure is of military interest" (quoted in Braffman-Miller, 1995, p. 6). The doctors did not use this procedure to treat tumors. Instead, they used it to study how radiation exposure might affect soldiers. These researchers also denied patients treatment for the nausea and vomiting that resulted from the radiation. These researchers instructed the hospital staff to ignore these symptoms: "DO NOT ASK THE PATIENT WHETHER HE HAS THESE SYMPTOMS" (see Figure 4.6). Instead, the staff were to record the symptoms' time, duration, and severity without treating the patient. Publicly, the researchers at the University of Cincinnati claimed the purpose of their research was to study ways to treat cancer. However, in a report to the Department of Defense, they wrote that the purpose of their study was to understand better the influence of radiation on "combat effectiveness of troops and to develop additional methods of diagnosis, prognosis, prophylaxis and treatment of [radiation] injuries" (quoted in Braffman-Miller, 1995, p. 5).

In 1966, Dr. George Shields and Dr. Thomas E. Gaffney at the University of Cincinnati formally questioned the purpose of the experiments. These doctors pointed out that the researchers deceived patients and were hiding the real purpose of their experiments. Their memos appear in Figures 4.7 and 4.8. Ultimately, the experiments were continued with some revisions.

From *Technical Communication* by Brenda Sims. Copyright © 2015 by Kendall Hunt Publishing Company. Reprinted by permission.

Instructions to the Hospital Staff at the University of Cincinnati

INSTRUCTIONS FOR RECORDING OF SYMPTOMS
FOLLOWING IRRADIATION

DEPARTMENT OF RADIOLOGY
GENERAL HOSPITAL

Date: _____

PATIENT_____ NO. _____ WARD _____

TIME OF THERAPY _____

This patient has just received total body radiation for therapeutic purposes. It is possible that the symptoms listed below may develop within the next several days. Please note carefully the time at which these symptoms develop and note their duration and severity.

DO NOT ASK THE PATIENT WHETHER HE HAS THESE SYMPTOMS

	Time of Onset Date Hr.	Duration	Severity
Anorexia			
Nausea			
Vomiting			
Abdominal Pain			
Diarrhea			
Weakness			
Prostration			
Mental Confusion			

E.L. Saenger, M.D., line 207
H. Perry, M.D., line 200

Source: Saenger, E. L. (n.d.) Research proposal for sub-task in nuclear weapons effect research. Retrieved September 30, 2001, from http://www.gwu.edu/~nsarchiv/radiation/dir/

Memo from Dr. George Shields (Reproduced verbatim)

TO: Dr. Edward A. Gall

FROM: Dr. George Shields

DATE: March 13, 1967

SUBJECT: Protection of Humans with Stored Autologous Marrow

I regret that I must withdraw myself from the subcommittee studying this proposal, for reasons of close professional and personal contact with the investigators and with some of the laboratory phases of this project. The following comments are sent to you in confidence, at your request.

This protocol is difficult to evaluate. The purpose of the study is obscure, as is the relationship of the experimental groups to the purposes. The significance of the study in relation to the health of the patients under study may be considerable if the investigators succeed in prolonging the lives of these patients with malignant disease, but the risk of treatment may be very high if the authors' hypothesis (that bone marrow transfusions will ameliorate bone marrow depression due to radiation) is incorrect. The radiation proposed has been documented in the authors' own series to cause a 25% mortality.

I recommend that this study be disapproved, because of the high risk of this level of radiation. Admittedly it is very difficult, in fact impossible, to balance potential hazard against potential benefit in experiments of this sort. The stakes are high. Our current mandate is that we evaluate the risks on some arbitrary scale. I believe a 25% mortality is too high (25% of 36 patients is 9 deaths), but this is of course merely an opinion.

If it is the consensus of the investigators and the review committee that a 25% mortality risk is not prohibitive, then the experiment could be reconsidered from the standpoint of informed consent - provided the patient is appraised of this risk in a quantative fashion. I believe that the conditions of informed consent will have been observed if the authors change "all patients are informed that a risk exists, but that all precautions to prevent untoward results will be taken" to the equivalent of "all patients are informed that a 1 in 4 chance of death within a few weeks due to treatment exists, etc."

Finally, although it is not our concern directly, a comment as to experimental design is indicated in this particular protocol. The authors' stated purposes are vague in the first page of the application, but on the last page three purposes are listed since it would require an untreated group and no reference has been made by the authors to such an untreated group of patients.

The second purpose can be fulfilled by this protocol only with the retrospective group (Group 1). The evaluation of bone marrow transfusion in the treatment of bone marrow depression would require a concomitant control group of patients treated only with radiation. It is apparent that the authors feel the radiation risk is too high to re-expose another group to this level of radiation without some effort at radio-protection, and therefore the authors have chosen to use the retrospective group as a control. There is considerable question whether this retrospective group will be entirely similar and therefore whether it will serve the second purpose.

The third purpose, "to determine whether autologous bone marrow therapy may play a role in treatment of bone marrow depression following acute radiation exposure in warfare or occupationally induced accidents," is not the subject of this experiment because normal individuals are not being tested. It is problematic whether the information gained in this study will apply to normal individuals following acute radiation exposure. Therefore it is my definite opinion that the third purpose of this experiment would not justify the risk entailed.

For these several reasons I feel that the experimental design is inadequate, and because of the high risk inherent in this level of radiation, I think experimental design should be a proper subject for our consideration in this instance.

Source: Department of Energy. (n.d.) Retrieved September 30, 2001, from http://www.gwu.edu/~nsarchiv/radiation/dir/

Memo from Dr. Thomas E. Gaffney (Reproduced verbatim)

To: Dr. Edward Gall, Chairman
         Clinical Research Committee

From: Dr. Thomas E. Gaffney,

Date: 4/17/67

I cannot recommend approval of the proposed study entitled "The Therapeutic Effect of Total Body Irradiation Followed by Infusion of Stored Autologous Marrow in Humans" for several reasons.

The stated goal of the study is to test the hypothesis that total body irradiation at a dose of 200 rad followed by infusion of stored autologous marrow is effective, palliative therapy for metastatic malignancy in human beings. I don't understand the rationale for this study. The applicants have apparently already administered 150-200 rad to some 18 patients with a variety of malignancies and to their satisfaction have not found a beneficial effect. In fact, as I understand it, they found considerable morbidity associated with this high dose radiation. Why is it now logical to expand this study?

Even if the study is expanded, its current design will not yield meaningful data. For instance, the applicants indicate their intention to evaluate the influence of 200 rad total body radiation on survival in patients with a variety of neoplasms. This "variety," or heterogeneity, will be present in a sample size of only 16 individuals. It will be difficult if not impossible to observe a beneficial effect in such a small sample containing a variety of diseases all of which share only CANCER in common.

This gross deficiency in design will almost certainly prevent making meaningful observations. When this deficiency in experimental method is placed next to their previously observed poor result and high morbidity with this type of treatment in a "variety of neoplasms," I think it is clear that the study as proposed should not be done.

I have the uneasy suspicion, shared up by the revised statement of objective, that this revised protocol is a subterfuge to allow the investigators to achieve the purpose described in their original application; mainly, to test the ability of autologous marrow to "take" in patients who have received high doses of total body radiation. This latter question may be an important one to answer but I can't justify 200 rad total body radiation simply for this purpose, "even in terminal case material".

I think there is sufficient question as to the propriety of these studies to warrant consideration by the entire Research Committee. I recommend therefore that this protocol and the previous one be circulated to all members of the Committee and that a meeting of the entire Committee be held to review this protocol prior to submitting a recommendation to the Dean.

Sincerely,

Thomas E. Gaffney, M.D.

Source: Department of Energy. (n.d.) Retrieved January 4, 2008, from http://www.gwu.edu/~nsarchiv/radiation/dir/mstreet/commeet/me

ENG 261 Ethics Writing Assignment

Find the code of conduct or code of ethics for your chosen career field. Using these guidelines as a basis, answer the following questions about a professional's behavior in the field.

1. Review the code of ethics, and then create your own list of what actions you believe the professional ethics to be describing.
2. What do the codes or guidelines suggest about the role of a professional in the workplace?
3. Are all the guidelines or terms clear to the reader?
4. Identify who would be decision makers for your field in the event of a conflict with an employee.

CHAPTER 3

Correspondence

We use written correspondence frequently in many aspects of the workplace to communicate valuable information to employees and customers. Communication via written correspondence will also happen from one company to the next and from company to community. We look to three forms of written communication, letter, memo, and electronic mail (which includes both e-mail and texts), within the workplace. Various types of information can be communicated in any one of these three forms and each form has unique purposes. As technical writers we need to know our audience and purpose, but we also need to understand the intent of each of these forms in order to choose the appropriate medium or form of communication for the situation.

Memo, Letter, E-mail Comparison: This table lists the generic tendencies for each form of correspondence, but all three forms are more or less interchangeable depending on the situation and organization.

	Memo	**Letter**	**E-mail**
Audience	Internal	External	Both
Formality	Informal	Formal	Informal
Social Cordialities (salutation, complimentary close, signature)	No	Yes	Yes

From *Business and Technical Writing* by Jeffrey Jablonski. Copyright © 2015 by Kendall Hunt Publishing Company. Reprinted by permission.

Each one of these choices, letter, memo, or e-mail, does follow a specific design or arrangement of information on the page. We have included a sample of each of these documents here for you to see. Please note the arrangement of information on the page for each of the forms.

Sample business letter

States Bank
Post Office Box 2130
New York, NY 11042

July 25, 2007

Sue M. Owens, Accounts Payable
Trico Cleaners
3211 N. Tower Ave.
Las Vegas, NV 89121

RE: Account number 198 211 14 2259 04

Dear Ms. Owens:

Your July 1, 2007 inquiry regarding your missing payment has been referred to my attention for review and reply.

A review of your account indicates that your May payments of $170.00 was misapplied.

I have corrected this error, and your payment has been credited to your account and back dated to reflect the correct receipt date. Any late charges incorrectly applied or adverse comments have been permanently removed from our records and those of credit reporting agencies used by National Bank.

Please accept my apologies for this error. If I can be of further assistance, please call the Customer Service Department at 1-800-226-5721, Monday through Friday, between 8 a.m. and 7 p.m., Eastern time.

Sincerely,

[signature]

Michelle Nicolette
Research Representative
CS002

Inside return address.

Recipient's address.

Subject line.

Salutation.

Opening that states purpose, in this case including a dated reference to the original correspondence.

Closing paragraph.

Complimentary close.

Signature block.

Sample Memo

In heading, use complete names and position titles.

Use a short, specific subject line.

Add an opening that states purpose clearly.

In body, break up big "chunks" of text into smaller, more readable paragraphs.

Use headings, lists, and emphasis (bold) to increase readability.

To: All employees, SeaCorp Inc.
CC: Roger May, VP Operations
FR: Elaine Darling, Chief Executive Officer *ED*
DT: January 4, 2004
RE: **E-Mail Use Policy**

The following policy covers appropriate use of any e-mail sent from a SeaCorp e-mail address and applies to all employees, vendors, and agents operating on behalf of SeaCorp.

Rationale
Our company needs to implement e-mail use guidelines for the following reasons:

1. **Professionalism:** by using proper e-mail language, our company will convey a more professional image and avoid tarnishing the company's public image.
2. **Efficiency:** e-mails that get to the point are much more effective than poorly worded e-mails.
3. **Protection from liability:** employee awareness of e-mail risks will protect our company from costly lawsuits.

E-mail Etiquette
It is far too easy to treat e-mail communications as an informal manner of communicating; however, it is a written record that is maintained in the ordinary course of business. You are reminded to maintain a business-like and professional decorum to your e-mail correspondence:

- Format e-mails as you would print memos.
- Use proper spelling, grammar, and punctuation.
- Never send messages containing derogatory, defamatory, obscene, or inappropriate content or attachments.

A simple test to bear in mind is: if you would not write the e-mail content in a formal business letter, then refrain from the user of such content in your e-mail messages.

Company Monitoring
All electronic mail messages are the property of SeaCorp, and employees should have no expectation of privacy whenever they store, send, or receive electronic mail using the company's electronic mail system. E-mail is a business record and may be subject to review by your manager, other employees, the courts, government agencies, litigants and other persons who are not the intended recipients of the e-mail. Deletion of a file on an employee's computer does not delete a record of the e-mail from the company's system.

Sample Memo *continued*

Notations can appear in either the heading (e.g., the "CC" line) or at the end of a memo.

Personal Use

Using a reasonable amount of SeaCorp resources for personal e-mail is acceptable, but non-work related e-mail must be saved in a separate folder from work related email. Sending chain letters or joke e-mails from a SeaCorp e-mail account is prohibited. Virus or other malware warnings and mass mailings from SeaCorp shall be approved by SeaCorp's VP of Operations before distribution. These restrictions also apply to the forwarding of mail received by a SeaCorp employee.

To sign a memo, either type or handwrite your name or initials after the closing. You can also initial by your name in the heading (as this sample does).

Enforcement

Any employee found to have violated this policy may be subject to disciplinary action, up to and including termination of employment.

Add a clear closing.

Questions about this policy should be directed to the VP of Operations.

Sample e-mail

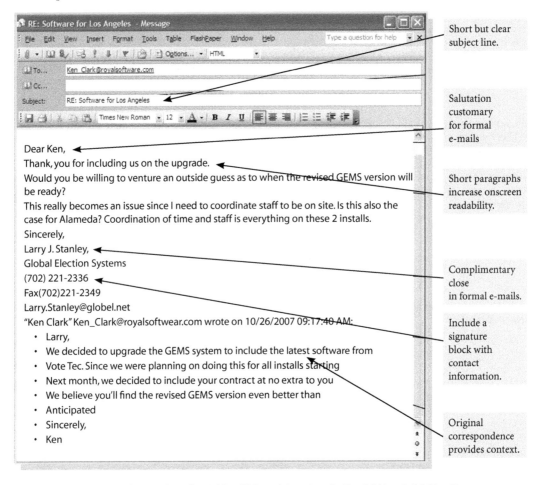

Short but clear subject line.

Salutation customary for formal e-mails

Short paragraphs increase onscreen readability.

Complimentary close in formal e-mails.

Include a signature block with contact information.

Original correspondence provides context.

The email content reads:

To... Ken_Clark@royalsoftware.com

Subject: RE: Software for Los Angeles

Dear Ken,

Thank, you for including us on the upgrade.

Would you be willing to venture an outside guess as to when the revised GEMS version will be ready?

This really becomes an issue since I need to coordinate staff to be on site. Is this also the case for Alameda? Coordination of time and staff is everything on these 2 installs.

Sincerely,

Larry J. Stanley,
Global Election Systems
(702) 221-2336
Fax(702)221-2349
Larry.Stanley@globel.net

"Ken Clark" Ken_Clark@royalsoftwear.com wrote on 10/26/2007 09:17:40 AM:

- Larry,
- We decided to upgrade the GEMS system to include the latest software from
- Vote Tec. Since we were planning on doing this for all installs starting
- Next month, we decided to include your contract at no extra to you
- We believe you'll find the revised GEMS version even better than
- Anticipated
- Sincerely,
- Ken

From *Business and Technical Writing* by Jeffrey Jablonski. Copyright © 2015 by Kendall Hunt Publishing Company. Reprinted by permission.

In addition to the specific format, writers need to concentrate on the style and tone of the messages. A letter, memo, or e-mail is a representation of the company. All communication needs to reflect the appropriate information and style for the situation. Messages that are communicated badly may result in employee misunderstandings or misuse, or even loss of a potential or existing customer.

1. **Passive and Impersonal Style**. Filled with **jargon** and difficult to read. Ineffective for routine correspondence as in the following example.

Dear Mr. Smith:

Per your letter of April 7, 20xx, enclosed please find the information in reference to our company that will help in optimizing your choices to build a website. Prices charged are in line with other designers of similar background and experience.

The company objective is to develop end-to-end robust solutions through continued focus on core competencies: Website development, hosting, and maintenance; full access to PHP and CGI; and, of course, SSL encryption. It is believed that the customer deserves the highest quality products and services possible. Through continued expansion of the company's staff and through application of corporate quality programs, such as benchmarking, our establishment of superior processes in each of the core competencies excels over our competitors.

Continued expansion into new, profitable markets will enable the company to provide clients with value-added services and turnkey solutions that will translate into client satisfaction.

Please find herein the company's packages that will endeavor to help the client learn more about the company's superior capabilities and its motivated professional team.

If you have any questions or concerns regarding the above, please feel free to contact Joanne Jones, at 800-543-6677, ext. 213. It is toll free for your convenience.

Very truly and obediently yours,

EXAMPLES OF LETTERS IN THREE WRITING STYLES *continued*

2. **Modern Business Style.** Uses active voice, strong verbs, short sentences.

Dear Mr. Smith:

Thank you for inquiring about our Web services. Our company specializes in creating websites. Your satisfaction is our priority. We work on projects of any size from large to small. Our prices range from $60 an hour for basic logo design to $100 an hour for designing and implementing a full-featured website.

Our staff includes seven Web designers who will turn your image of a perfect website into reality. We can fulfill any of your Web design needs from developing high-end graphics and animation to incorporating video and sound. We realize that your organization may not yet be clear on what your Web needs are. Our talented staff will work with you to guide you in the right direction.

I have enclosed a brochure that explains the four website design packages we offer. Choose the one that is right for your needs, then give us a toll-free call any time at 800-543-6677. We will be glad to set up a free consultation.

Sincerely,

EXAMPLES OF LETTERS IN THREE WRITING STYLES *continued*

3. **Informal/Colorful Style.** Good for communicating with people you know well or for communicating good news to those you are familiar with.

Dear Jack,

Thanks for asking about our Web design services. We have a full range of services and can provide you with just about anything you want in the way of website design. Our prices are competitive. We charge $60 an hour for basic logo design and up to $100 an hour to design and get your site up and running.

As you know, we have seven talented designers who work on all projects. I have included a brochure that explains the various website design packages we offer. If you have a clear idea of what you want on your site, shoot your ideas over via e-mail to bwo@clear.com or give me a call at 800-657-8000. If you're not sure exactly what you want from a website, just give me a call, and we can set up a consult.

It's great to hear from you, and I look forward to working with you again.

Sincerely,

Rejection Slip #1

FROM: Joseph Milton, fiction editor JM
TO: Henry Waters
DATE: 12/18/13
SUBJ: Recent submission

Dear Mr. Waters,
We regret that your short story *Aliens Live in my Basement* does not meet our needs.

Rejection Slip #2

FROM: Joseph Milton, fiction editor JM
TO: Henry Waters
DATE: 12/18/13
SUBJ: Recent submission

Dear Mr. Waters,
Thank you for submitting your short story *Aliens Live in my Basement*. Though it does not meet our needs at this time, we believe the story has potential if developed. Plus you have skill in writing dialogue. Please continue to submit stories. Good luck.

Examples of E-mail Tone

Authoritative and Emotional

FROM: Alex Bender, sales vp   AB
TO: Amy Correia, sales associate
DATE: 12/18/13SUBJ:
Urgent information about health package

Amy,
It is imperative that you attend Tuesday afternoon's meeting in the conference room regarding health package updates.

Moral and Ethical

FROM: Alex Bender, sales vp AB
TO: Amy Correia, sales associate
DATE: 12/18/13
SUBJ: Urgent information about health package

Amy,
It is highly recommended that you attend Tuesday afternoon's meeting in the conference room regarding health package updates. The company wants you to have the best package possible and of course it is in your own best interests to want to enjoy good health. See you Tuesday.

Logical

FROM: Alex Bender, sales vp AB
TO: Amy Correia, sales associate
DATE: 12/18/13
SUBJ: Urgent information about health package

Amy,
Starting Jan. 1, 2014, monthly health package premium will increase 5.5%. In addition, several benefits are being cut back and others added.

We want you to have the best benefits package available and know what you are paying for. The Human Resource director as well as a corporate health package expert will be on hand to answer questions and concerns.

Note the similar but engaging words in each subject line that would prompt quick reading, as well as the difference in tone of each e-mail.

From *Technical Writing in the Workplace* by Harvey Ussach. Copyright © 2014 by Kendall Hunt Publishing Company. Reprinted by permission.

DIRECT STRATEGY, GOOD-NEWS LETTER (POORLY-WRITTEN VERSION)

Advanced Energies
22 Harris Drive
Houston, TX 77003
(713) 436-9102

April 2, 201X

1078 First St.
Austin, TX 78702

Dear Chao:

It was a pleasure visiting with you on March 15. Advanced Energies is a leader in the energy industry, and I am certain you were impressed with all you learned about us during your visit. While Advanced Energies has focused predominately on oil and natural gas exploration in the past, we are currently entering the solar energy market with plans for expansion. With all this growth and diversity, we are adding to our ranks of employees and that's where you come in. We would like you to come to work for us.

We will start you out with a two-day orientation next month. Then, we will place you in one of the areas where we have the most need of help. I hope you are flexible in regard to the type of work you do. During your orientation we will discuss your starting pay rate and benefits package.

See you in May.

Very truly yours,

Juan Lopez
Legal Department

Enclosures: 3

DIRECT STRATEGY, GOOD-NEWS LETTER (IMPROVED VERSION)

Advanced Energies
22 Harris Drive
Houston, TX 77003
(713) 436-9102

April 2, 201X

Mr. Chao Yung
1078 First St.
Austin, TX 78702

Dear Chao:

We are pleased to offer you the position of Research Director in the Legal Department at Advanced Energies. You have the exact qualifications and personality we hoping to find in a candidate for this position and believe we are a good fit for you also.

As mentioned during our March 24 interview, orientation will take place on April 17–18. Plan to arrive at my office (2024B, second floor, Progressive Tower) at 9 a.m. on April 17. We have much information to share with you, and know you will have questions. Please develop a list of questions you have and e-mail it to me by April 16 so I have time to review it prior to meeting with you. In addition, please review the attached benefits information and be prepared to make selections from the benefits options. Finally, please review the Legal Department's policy handbook, which can be found at AEpolicies@lgldept.com prior to April 17.

We are excited about having you as a member of the Advanced Energies team. During the upcoming days, please contact me at (713) 436-9102, ext. 32 or at juan.lopez27@ AE.org. See you on the 17th.

Sincerely,

Juan Lopez
Legal Department

Enclosures: 3

DIRECT STRATEGY, GOOD-NEWS LETTER (POORLY-WRITTEN VERSION)

Hanley Farm Equipment
213 Lima Avenue
Findlay, OH 45840
(419) 724-6153

June 12, 201X

Mr. Robert G. Conway
CR347
Arcadia, OH 44804

Dear Mr. Conway:

We are pleased with your interest in the Global Star global positioning system. Our Global Star global positioning system is revolutionizing the farming industry! Our global positioning system can save users enough money to pay it off quickly with increased profits. This is why we are happy to grant you credit to purchase the equipment you expressed interest in.

Our field representative, Tom Holman, will call you soon to get you on his installation schedule. Following this initial meeting, contact Tom any time you have questions.

Thanks for giving us your business.

Cordially,

Sharon Tyler
Accounts Manager

From *Communicating in Business* by Robert Insley. Copyright © 2014 by Kendall Hunt Publishing Company. Reprinted by permission.

In a correspondence with a positive tone, often it is tempting to rush through or oversimplify the work, knowing that it will not be met with any anticipated resistance or concerns. However, while brevity is important to clarify your purpose, this should not excuse a lack of detail or seeming redundancy in style. Though your purpose is to convey good news, doing so in a short simplistic fashion may convey an unintended sense of disinterest or a lack of effort.

Rework the sample letter provided on page 35 to Mr. Robert G. Conway of Hanley Farm Equipment as a more effective and improved correspondence in phrasing and style. Do not change the message (or purpose) of the letter, but with consideration to the audience thereof, rephrase how the provided letter delivers this message.

Note: Your work should still be a letter in format—do not select a different formatting or style for the correspondence.

Hint: You may need to "invent" some information here regarding this topic, which is permissible for this exercise.

Hint: No aspect of the heading of the letter should be altered.

INDIRECT STRATEGY, NEGATIVE-NEWS LETTER
(POORLY-WRITTEN VERSION)

Sunny Valley Resort
14 Timberlane Rd.
Sante Fe, NM 87594
(505) 331-2424

December 2, 201X

Mr. Nicholas P. Brunsell
2400 Brumly St., Apt. 27
Santa Fe, NM 87504

Dear Nick,

The weather sure hasn't been very cooperative this fall. Here we are in early December, and we've had only one decent snowfall. It dropped enough snow for us to open a few runs, but we are nowhere close to full operation. We are really hurting because of this situation. This is not what you want to hear because the situation has caused us to initiate a hiring freeze.

Conditions will change if we get some more snow soon, but I am not holding out much hope with all this talk about global warming. If by some miracle we do get two or more significant snowfalls soon, everything will be good for us, and we will consider hiring additional help. I guess we will see what happens.

Sorry to have to share bad news. Thanks for your interest in working for the Sunny Valley Resort.

Sincerely,

Ron Baker
Operating Manager

INDIRECT STRATEGY, NEGATIVE-NEWS LETTER
(IMPROVED VERSION)

Sunny Valley Resort
14 Timberlane Rd.
Sante Fe, NM 87594
(505) 331-2424

December 2, 201X

Mr. Nicholas X. Jackson
2400 Brumly St., Apt. 27
Santa Fe, New Mexico 87504

Dear Nick,

We have finally been blessed with a long-overdue snowfall. For snowboarding enthusiasts, such as yourself, this is certainly good news.

We plan to open approximately half of our beginners and intermediate runs and one-quarter of our advanced runs this coming Saturday, with the hope that there will be enough new snowfall during the next three weeks to open the remaining runs by Christmas. In the meantime, we plan to supplement as much as possible with manmade powder. Even then, at least one significant snowfall will be needed to ready the remaining runs. At the time we are able to open at least 80 percent of the runs, we will be able to hire on additional help. Until then, the volume of business will not support hiring additional seasonal staff. Despite this temporary setback, if you are still interested in working at the Sunny Valley Resort this winter, please e-mail me at RonBaker12@sunnyvalley.org. As soon as snow conditions are right to support opening most of the remaining runs, we will bring you onboard. If for some reason this doesn't occur, we would like you to consider joining our summer whitewater rafting staff. Doing so would then secure you a guaranteed position with us for next winter.

I believe you will be a valuable member of Sunny Valley team and look forward to working with you. Please stay in touch.

Sincerely,

Ron Baker
Operating Manager

From *Communicating in Business* by Robert Insley. Copyright © 2014 by Kendall Hunt Publishing Company. Reprinted by permission.

INDIRECT STRATEGY, NEGATIVE-NEWS LETTER
(POORLY-WRITTEN VERSION)

DD&D Corporation
10 Franklin Avenue
Boston, MA 02103
(617) 558-9867

February 16, 201X

Ms. Nancee L. Reid
457 Hartford Lane
Boston, MA 02105

Dear Ms. Reid:

This letter is being written to inform you that DD&D Corporation has no interest in taking part in your corporate sales projections research project. We will not grant you permission to access our sales projections figures.

In fact, our company has a policy that prohibits its participation in external research projects such as yours. If we were to provide sales projection figures to you for your proposed project, it would cause us numerous problems because other researchers would then expect the same treatment!

We are sorry we couldn't meet your request. However, if we can help you in any other way, please let us know.

Cordially,

Jeff Oliver
Public Relations Manager

From *Communicating in Business* by Robert Insley. Copyright © 2014 by Kendall Hunt Publishing Company. Reprinted by permission.

It is important to convey an effective, inoffensive tone while still delivering an honest and clear message in a negative communication. While maintaining a correct format for the letter, rework the sample letter provided on page 39 to Ms. Nancee L. Reid of the DD&D Corporation as a more effective and improved correspondence in phrasing and style. Do not change the message (or purpose) of the letter, but with consideration to the audience thereof, rephrase how the provided letter delivers this message.

Note: Your work should still be a letter in format—do not select a different formatting or style for the correspondence.

Hint: No aspect of the heading of the letter should be altered.

E-mailhead

To: recipient@byco.com
From: Mia Deal (mdeal@herco.com)
Subject: Offer to Purchase Smartboards

Her Company Inc.
3024 Main Street
Chicago, IL 54890

Dear Mr. Brown:
text
text
Sincerely,
Mia Deal
Marketing Manager
(mdeal@herco.com)

SUPERIOR BABY STROLLERS

698 West 21st Street, New York, NY 10016
555-555-5555

November 16, 2013

Jane Wilkins
25-26 141st Street
Bayside, NY 22222

Dear Valued Customer:

Thank you for being a good customer in the past. Our records show you purchased a crib and a highchair just two years ago. We hope you are satisfied with those items. Superior Baby Strollers prides itself on manufacturing quality products and we make every effort to correct problems.

You purchased BabySafe Stroller #1224, in blue with yellow birds, from Baby Depot in Bayside, on September 30. When we checked with the store manager—we are always in contact with our retailers—he reported that when you returned the stroller he noticed the stroller frame and braces had sagged too much. It turned out that the stroller had borne unusual weight, like something was moved in it. For that reason, he could not replace or reimburse the stroller.

Mrs. Wilkins, BabySafe strollers are made of top quality metal and fabric and put to extreme tests in our lab, but we find in this case that improper use of the stroller invalidated the warranty. We cannot take it back.

However, we value your business and want you to be a good customer of ours, so we are enclosing several discount coupons on strollers and other products at Baby Depot.

Sincerely,

Mark Halprin,
Senior Product Manager

cc. Baby Depot
encl. (3) discount coupons

From *Technical Writing in the Workplace* by Harvey Ussach. Copyright © 2014 by Kendall Hunt Publishing Company. Reprinted by permission.

CHAPTER 4

Document Design and Graphics

Document with No Headings or Design Elements

Canine Epilepsy

Epilepsy is a disorder characterized by recurrent seizures. Seizures, also known as fits or convulsions, occur when an area of nerve cells in the brain becomes overexcitable. This area is often called a seizure focus. The mechanism responsible for developing this focus is unknown.

A dog can inherit or acquire canine epilepsy. Inherited epilepsy affects about 1% of the canine population. Breeds which may inherit epilepsy include the beagle, Belgian shepherd, German shepherd, dachshund, and keeshond. Researchers also suspect a genetic factor in the following breeds: cocker spaniel, collie, golden retriever, Labrador retriever, Irish setter, miniature schnauzer, poodle, Saint Bernard, Siberian husky, and wire-haired fox terrier.

Acquired epilepsy may occur months to years after an injury or illness that causes brain damage. In many cases, the dog is completely normal except for occasional seizures. Causes of acquired epilepsy include trauma, infection, poisons, hypoxia (lack of oxygen), and low blood sugar concentrations.

A dog with inherited epilepsy has generalized seizures that affect its entire brain and body. The dog usually falls on its side and displays paddling motions with all four limbs. During or immediately after the seizures, the dog may also exhibit loss of consciousness (i.e., the dog will not respond when you call its name), excessive drooling, and urinating or passing of feces. The seizure of inherited epilepsy usually occurs between the ages of 1 and 3 years. Seizures that occur before 6 months or after 5 years of age probably result from acquired epilepsy.

A dog with acquired epilepsy has partial seizures. A partial seizure affects only one part of the body, and the dog may not lose consciousness. During a partial seizure, the dog may exhibit turning of the head to one side, muscular contractions of one or both legs on the same side of the body, or bending of the body to one side. These signs are localizing because they help to determine the location of the seizure focus in the brain. The localizing sign may occur only briefly, after which the seizure becomes generalized. If the seizure becomes generalized, you or your veterinarian may have difficulty distinguishing between acquired and inherited epilepsy. The first seizure may occur at any age.

You can treat epilepsy by giving anticonvulsant medication orally several times a day. This treatment is effective in 60 to 70% of epileptic dogs. Unfortunately, the medication will not completely eliminate the seizures. Instead, the medication reduces the frequency, severity, and duration of the seizures. Most veterinarians recommend that dogs receive the anticonvulsant medication when the seizures occur more often than once every 6 weeks or when severe clusters of seizures occur more often than once every 2 months. To successfully treat epilepsy, you must consistently give the medication as directed by the veterinarian and continue the medication without interruption. If you discontinue the medication, status epilepticus could occur, resulting in the dog's death. Status epilepticus is a series of seizures without periods of consciousness. If this condition occurs, contact a veterinarian immediately.

Document Broken Up with Headings and Design Elements

Canine Epilepsy

Epilepsy is a disorder characterized by recurrent seizures. Seizures, also known as fits or convulsions, occur when an area of nerve cells in the brain becomes overexcitable. This area is often called a seizure focus. The mechanism responsible for developing this focus is unknown.

Types of Canine Epilepsy

A dog can inherit or acquire canine epilepsy. Inherited epilepsy affects about 1% of the canine population. Breeds which may inherit epilepsy include the beagle, Belgian shepherd, German shepherd, dachshund, and keeshond. Researchers also suspect a genetic factor in the following breeds: cocker spaniel, collie, golden retriever, Labrador retriever, Irish setter, miniature schnauzer, poodle, Saint Bernard, Siberian husky, and wire-haired fox terrier. Acquired epilepsy may occur months to years after an injury or illness that causes brain damage. In many cases, the dog is completely normal except for occasional seizures. Causes of acquired epilepsy include trauma, infection, poisons, hypoxia (lack of oxygen), and low blood sugar concentrations.

Characteristics of Inherited Epilepsy

A dog with inherited epilepsy has generalized seizures that affect its entire brain and body. The dog usually falls on its side and displays paddling motions with all four limbs. During or immediately after the seizures, the dog may also exhibit some or all of the following signs:

- loss of consciousness (i.e., the dog will not respond when you call its name)
- excessive drooling
- urinating or passing of feces.

The seizure usually lasts no longer than 1 or 2 minutes. The first seizure of inherited epilepsy usually occurs between the ages of 1 and 3 years. Seizures that occur before 6 months or after 5 years of age probably result from acquired epilepsy.

Characteristics of Acquired Epilepsy

A dog with acquired epilepsy has partial seizures. A partial seizure affects only one part of the body, and the dog may not lose consciousness. During a partial seizure, the dog may exhibit one or more of the following localizing signs:

- turning of the head to one side
- muscular contractions of one or both legs on the same side of the body
- bending of the body to one side.

These signs are localizing because they help to determine the location of the seizure focus in the brain. The localizing sign may occur only briefly, after which the seizure becomes generalized. If the seizure becomes generalized, you or your veterinarian may have difficulty distinguishing between acquired and inherited epilepsy. The first seizure may occur at any age.

Treatment of Canine Epilepsy

You can treat epilepsy by giving anticonvulsant medication orally several times a day. This treatment is effective in 60 to 70% of epileptic dogs. Unfortunately, the medication will not completely eliminate the seizures. Instead, the medication reduces the frequency, severity, and duration of the seizures. Most veterinarians recommend that dogs receive the anticonvulsant medication when the seizures occur more often than once every 6 weeks or when sever clusters of seizures occur more often than once every 2 months.

To successfully treat epilepsy, you must
- consistently give the medication as directed by the veterinarian
- continue the medication without interruption.

If you discontinue the medication, status epilepticus could occur, resulting in the dog's death. Status epilepticus is a series of seizures without periods of consciousness. If this condition occurs, contact a veterinarian immediately.

Document Design and Graphics

As you can see from the example "Canine Epilepsy" on the first two pages of this chapter, document design can create a big impact on any form of communication. Specifically document design can make a communication more readable and can also influence retention of the information presented. Let's face it, most people do not read an entire document from the beginning to the ending, or read it carefully to understand every word. Technical documents are not an exception to this idea, and many people in the workplace are more likely NOT to read a complete document. As writers, we must work with that idea and provide information in accessible forms for specific readers.

Document design can include really simple ideas such as inserting headings with our writing and creating lists of information rather than writing complete paragraphs. We can also look to the use of graphics and color to improve a document for the reader. While the use of graphics and color may attract a reader to the page, it can also help a reader to remember or retain the information for future use. You can see many examples of the various ways a writer can improve a document within this chapter and your instructor will discuss the many types with you.

Whatever you choose to do with information when preparing a document, you must always consider the audience who will be reading the document and your purpose for creating the document. Who is the reader and what do you want the reader to know or do should be your first concern and should guide your decisions on the best way to prepare the design.

Aligning Lists Correctly

Incorrectly Aligned	**Correctly Aligned**
Text	Text
• subtext	• subtext
• subtext	• subtext
Text 2	Text 2
• subtext 2	• subtext 2
• subtext 2	• subtext 2

From *Technical Communication* by Brenda Sims. Copyright © 2015 by Kendall Hunt Publishing Company. Reprinted by permission.

Headers and Footers

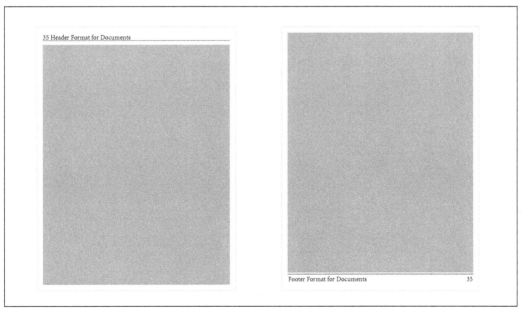

From *Technical Communication* by Brenda Sims. Copyright © 2015 by Kendall Hunt Publishing Company. Reprinted by permission.

Three Formats for Effective Headings

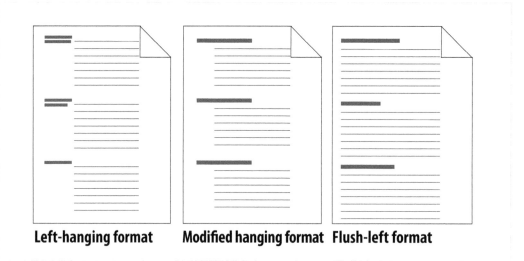

Left-hanging format   **Modified hanging format**   **Flush-left format**

From *Technical Communication* by Brenda Sims. Copyright © 2015 by Kendall Hunt Publishing Company. Reprinted by permission.

Using White Space to Highlight Bullets

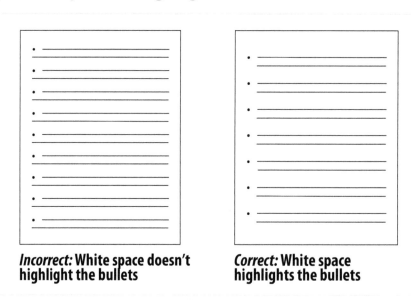

Incorrect: **White space doesn't highlight the bullets**   *Correct:* **White space highlights the bullets**

From *Technical Communication* by Brenda Sims. Copyright © 2015 by Kendall Hunt Publishing Company. Reprinted by permission.

Effective Use of Color, Headings and Typeface

Chapter 3
Keeping the Participants Interested

Once you have your equipment in place and you have planned and rehearsed your presentation, you're almost ready. However, you can improve your chances for a successful presentation by understanding ways to keep your participants interested (and awake). In other words, put yourself in your participants' seat! This chapter will present some strategies to help you keep participants interested:

Modified hanging headings help readers locate Information.

- Give participants only the information they need.
- Anticipate participants' needs and questions.
- Provide participants with a "road map" and examples.
- Help participants enjoy your presentation.

The designers effectively use color to emphasize the headings. Notice that a colorblind reader could still easily locate the headings because they appear in boldface type as well as color.

Strategy 1: Give Participants Only the Information They Need

Keep your presentation short and simple. Participants want to hear only the information they need and no more. As you prepare for your presentation, consider the following:

- **Listening to information takes twice as long as reading that same information.** Thus, if you can read 10 pages in 8 minutes, your participants can comprehend the same information in about 16 minutes.

The text aligns after the bullets.

- **Condense your presentation into a few points.** Don't try to give participants every bit of information you have about a topic or all the tiny details. Instead, select the key points and present those. If necessary, you can refer your participants to the quick reference cards or to other printed handouts.
- **Plan the presentation to take slightly less then the allotted time.** Look for ways to tighten your presentation, so you have time for the participants to ask questions. Your participants will prefer a presentation that is a couple of minutes short rather than a presentation that exceeds the allotted time.

The designers have used a sans serif typeface for the headings and a serif typeface for the text.

Strategy 2: Anticipate Participants' Needs and Questions

As you are preparing and even as you are speaking, think about what participants already know and what they will want to know about the topic.

- **Customize your presentation according to what you know about your participants.** You will always begin your presentation with the same four databases: Project Description, Project Contacts, Specifications, and

From *Technical Communication* by Brenda Sims. Copyright © 2015 by Kendall Hunt Publishing Company. Reprinted by permission.

Selecting the Appropriate Graphic

Purpose	Types of Graphic	Best Use of the Graphic
Illustrate quantitative (numerical) information	Bar graphs	• show comparisons of approximate values • summarize relationships among data
	Line graphs	• show trends (changes) over time, cost, or other variable
	Pie charts	• show the relationship of the parts to a whole
	Pictographs	• summarize statistical information for general readers
	Tables	• summarize and categorize large amounts of numerical data
Show relationships of qualitative (not numerical) information	Organizational charts	• show the hierarchy in an organization or company • show how something is organized
	Diagrams	• show a sequence of events
	Tables	• show relationships and summarize data
Show instructions and processes	Flow charts	• explain a process or a sequence of events or steps
	Tables	• organize information • indicate troubleshooting and frequently asked questions with answers
	Line drawings	• show a realistic, but simplified view of what something looks like
	Diagrams	• demonstrate how to do something • show where something is located to complete a task or understand a process
Show what something looks like	Line drawings	• show a representation of what something will or does look like
	Photos	• give a realistic picture • show exactly what something looks like
	Screen shots	• show what appears on a computer monitor

From *Technical Communication* by Brenda Sims. Copyright © 2015 by Kendall Hunt Publishing Company. Reprinted by permission.

Multiple-Bar Graph

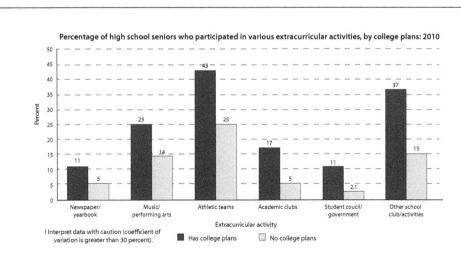

Percentage of high school seniors who participated in various extracurricular activities, by college plans: 2010

! Interpret data with caution (coefficient of variation is greater than 30 percent).

■ Has college plans   ☐ No college plans

Source: Aud, S., et al. (2012). *The condition of education 2012* (Report No. NCEDS 2012-045). p. 71. Retrieved from National Center for Education Statistics Website: http://nces.ed.gov/pubs2012/2012045_1.pdf

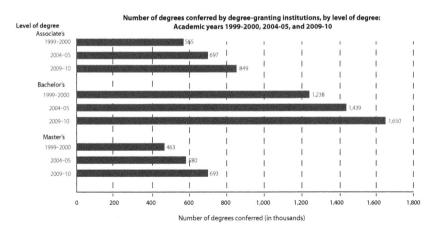

Number of degrees conferred by degree-granting institutions, by level of degree: Academic years 1999-2000, 2004-05, and 2009-10

Source: Aud, S., et al. (2012). *The condition of education 2012* (Report No. NCES 2012-045). p. 113. Retrieved from National Center for Education Statistics Website: http://nces.ed.gov/pubs2012/2012045_4.pdf

Line Graph that Shows Change Over Time

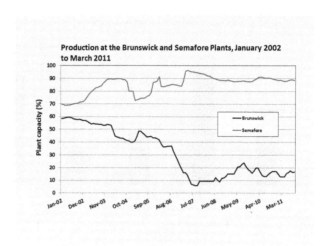

From *Technical Communication* by Brenda Sims. Copyright © 2015 by Kendall Hunt Publishing Company. Reprinted by permission.

Pie Chart

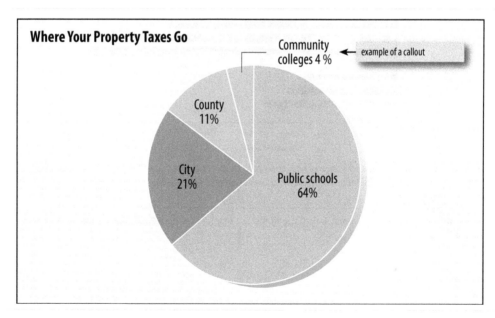

From *Technical Communication* by Brenda Sims. Copyright © 2015 by Kendall Hunt Publishing Company. Reprinted by permission.

The Same Data Presented in Different Graphics

Average Annual Salary and Average Beginning Salary for Public Elementary and Secondary School Teachers (in 1993 Dollars): Selected School Years Ending 1960–93

School year ending	All teachers	Elementary teachers	Secondary teachers	Beginning salary*
1960	$ 24,599	$ 23,712	$ 25,983	—
1964	28,127	27,235	29,398	—
1968	31,584	30,669	32,729	—
1972	34,127	33,138	35,273	$ 24,128
1976	32,876	32,041	33,755	23,104
1980	29,766	29,019	30,678	20,504
1984	31,184	30,547	32,064	21,562
1988	35,017	34,373	35,974	23,968
1992	34,618	34,053	35,421	24,001
1993	35,873	35,308	36,609	23,969

— Not available
* Beginning teacher salary is for the calendar year.

Source: Smith, T.M., et al. (1994). *The condition of education 1994* (Report No. NCES 94-149). pp. 154, 155. Retrieved from National Center for Education Statistics Website: http://nces.ed.gov/pubs94/94149.pdf

From *Technical Communication* by Brenda Sims. Copyright © 2015 by Kendall Hunt Publishing Company. Reprinted by permission.

Quantitative Data Presented in a Table

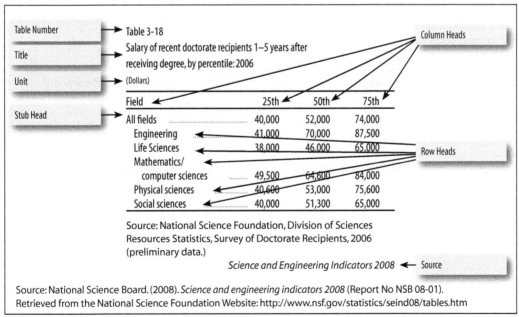

Source: National Science Foundation, Division of Sciences Resources Statistics, Survey of Doctorate Recipients, 2006 (preliminary data.)

Science and Engineering Indicators 2008

From *Technical Communication* by Brenda Sims. Copyright © 2015 by Kendall Hunt Publishing Company. Reprinted by permission.

Table Consisting of Words Instead of Numerical Data

How to Store Egg Products Safely		
Type of egg product	How long can you store the product in the refrigerator?	How long can you store the product in the freezer?
Raw eggs in shell	3 to 5 weeks	Do not freeze. (Beat yolks and whiles together before freezing)
Raw egg whites	2 to 4 days	12 months
Raw egg yolks	2 to 4 days	Do not freeze
Hard-boiled eggs	7 days	Do not freeze
Egg substitutes, liquid (unopened)	10 days	12 months
Egg substitutes, liquid (opened)	3 days	Do not freeze
Egg substitutes, frozen (unopened)	7 days after thawing or refer to the "use-by" date	12 months
Egg substitutes, Frozen (opened)	3 days after thawing or refer to the "use-by" date	Do not freeze
Casseroles containing eggs	3 to 4 days	2 to 3 months after baking. Do not freeze unbaked casseroles containing eggs
Eggnog (commercial)	3 to 5 days	6 months
Eggnog (homemade)	2 to 5 days	Do not freeze
Pies-Pumpkin and pecan	3 to 4 days	1 to 2 months after baking
Pies-Custard and chiffon	3 to 4 days	Do not freeze
Quiche	3 to 4 days	1 to 2 months after baking

Presenting Visual Information with Combined Graphics

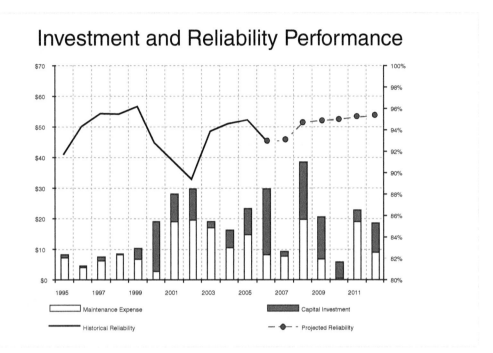

From *Technical Communication* by Brenda Sims. Copyright © 2015 by Kendall Hunt Publishing Company. Reprinted by permission.

TIPS for Using Color to Enhance and Clarify Graphics

- **Don't overuse color** (Parker & Berry, 1998). If you use too many colors in a document or on one page, you won't impress your readers and you may confuse them. Make sure each color has a purpose.
- **Choose colors that will give your documents a unified look.** Use a color wheel such as the one in Figure 4.1. When selecting colors for a document, pick corresponding colors—three or four adjacent colors on the wheel (Parker & Berry, 1998). For example, you might select blue, green, and yellow.
- **Choose a triad of colors to create contrast in your graphics.** A triad of colors is three colors that are relatively equidistant from each other on the color wheel—such as yellow, red, and blue (Parker & Berry, 1998).
- **To create an effective contrast, choose colors that stand out against the background.** For example, don't use a shade of red on a red background; not all readers can easily distinguish among shades of red (see Figure 4.2). Use contrasting colors such as black and red.
- **If your readers associate a color with a particular meaning, use that color as your readers expect.** For example, U.S. readers associate red with danger or warning and yellow with caution. However, for readers outside the United States, these colors have different meanings.
- **Use bright colors to make objects look bigger.** For example, look at the stars in Figure 4.3. The stars are the same size; however, the yellow star looks larger than the blue star.
- **Make sure the text stands out from the background.** If you use a dark background, make the text white or another light color (see Figure 4.4).

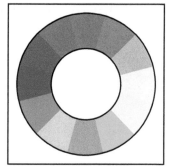

Figure 4.1 The Color Wheel

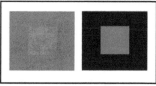

Figure 4.2 Using Color to Create Contrast

Figure 4.3 Bright Colors Make Objects Look Larger

Figure 4.4 Make Sure Text Stands Out

Flow Chart

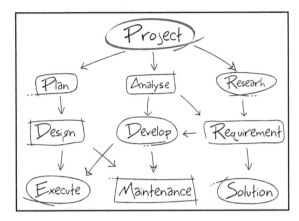

© 2014 Vectomart. Used under license from Shutterstock, Inc.

Gantt Chart

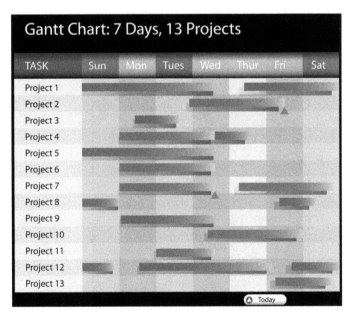

© 2014 John T Takai. Used under license from Shutterstock, Inc.

From *Technical Writing in the Workplace* by Harvey Ussach. Copyright © 2014 by Kendall Hunt Publishing Company. Reprinted by permission.

Cutaway View

© 2014 Pixsooz. Used under license from Shutterstock, Inc.

Exploded Diagram

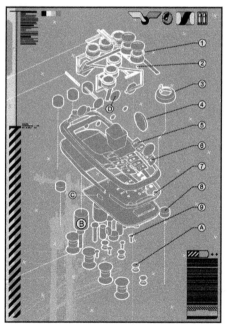

© 2014 LANBO. Used under license from Shutterstock, Inc.

Schematic

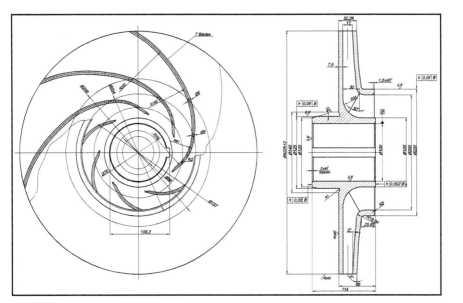

© 2014 cherezoff. Used under license from Shutterstock, Inc.

From *Technical Writing in the Workplace* by Harvey Ussach. Copyright © 2014 by Kendall Hunt Publishing Company. Reprinted by permission.

Creating Visual Information

Labor market indicators for recent S&E degree recipients up to 5 years after receiving degree, by field: 2008						
			Highest degree Field			
Indicator and degree	All S&E fields	Computer/ mathematical sciences	Biological/ agricultural/ environmental life sciences	Physical sciences	Social Sciences	Engineering
Unemployment rate (%)						
All degree levels	4.6	3.2	5.1	3.4	6.1	2.0
Bachelor's	5.3	3.2	6.0	3.9	6.7	2.1
Master's	2.9	3.5	2.4	2.5	3.5	2.0
Doctorate	1.5	0.3	2.1	2.5	1.2	1.0
Involuntary out of field rate (%)						
All degree levels	7.9	4.0	7.6	5.6	12.0	2.4
Bachelor's	9.7	5.4	9.1	7.6	13.6	2.5
Master's	3.5	0.7	4.1	1.8	6.1	2.6
Doctorate	1.5	0.9	1.2	3.1	1.9	0.8
Median annual salary($)						
All degree levels	42,000	55,000	34,000	40,000	36,000	63,000
Bachelor's	39,800	51,000	30,000	32,000	34,000	59,000
Master's	57,000	72,000	44,000	47,000	43,000	70,000
Doctorate	65,000	80,000	50,000	67,000	60,000	86,0000

Notes: Median annual salaries are rounded to nearest $1,000. All degree levels includes professional degrees not broken out separately. Includes degrees, earned from October 2003 to October 2008. Involuntarily out-of-field rate is proportion of individuals employed in job not related to field of highest degree because job in that field was not available.

Source: National Science Foundation, National Center for Science and Engineering Statistics, Scientists and Engineers Statistical Data System (SESTAT) (2008), http://sestat.nsf.gov

Science and Engineering Indicators 2012

Using the above table as a data source, create various tables and charts that relate specific information. These charts can be completed using MS Word. Be sure to correctly label all parts of the chart/graph or table that you create. Some items may ask you to interpret the data you have just illustrated.

1. Create a pie chart that illustrates the unemployment rate in % for Social Science majors divided by the degree the individual has earned.

2. Using a multiple line graph compare the median annual salary for Physical Science, Engineering and Computer/Mathematical Sciences for each degree level. What conclusions can you make about these careers based on this data?

3. Create a pie chart showing the unemployment rates for each of the five fields listed in the column heads.

4. Compare the amount of unemployment for Master's Degree and Doctoral degree levels for all career fields using a multiple bar graph. What trend do you notice?

5. Create a table that illustrates the difference in involuntary out-of-field rate to the unemployment rate by degree and by field.

6. Compare the unemployment rate for Master's and Doctorate degrees for all majors listed using a double line graph. What advice would you give to a degree seeking student in these areas?

7. Compare the median annual salaries for all science majors at the Bachelor's and Master's degree levels in a double bar chart.

8. Illustrate the annual median salaries of Computer/mathematical sciences, Physical Sciences and Social Sciences by degree level using a table.

9. Using a multiple line graph compare the unemployment rate for all S&E majors at all three degree levels to Physical Science and Engineering.

10. Compare the unemployment rate to the involuntary out-of-field rate for all degree levels for the majors listed here using a double line graph.

CHAPTER 5

Presentations

Often in the workplace situations arise in which information must be shared in an oral medium, as opposed to the written formats focused upon thus far in this text. While noticeable distinctions of course exist between written and oral styles of communication, there are also several similarities between these media.

For instance, whether composing a report or delivering a presentation, considering your *audience* and *purpose* (as discussed in Chapter 1) is still integral from the start. First determining what you look to achieve and to whom your work should be addressed is a key primary step. Therefore, organizing your presentation into the discussed introduction–body–conclusion format (also in Chapter 1) remains true here. In fact, in many regards, most of the prewriting considerations addressed here regarding reports apply also to preparing for a presentation.

Still, there are some unique considerations to preparing a presentation. The type(s) of oral presentation expected, the use of slideshows and other visual accompaniments, and audience involvement and interaction throughout the experience are some of the central concerns addressed throughout this chapter.

At some point in life, we have all experienced a presentation of some type: in the classroom, in a social setting, at work, or even for entertainment purposes. Likely some were enjoyable and beneficial, while others may have felt dull or pointless. That is because there is no one set, universal way to "best" deliver a presentation. Options exist—as with reports—and therefore mistakes can be made. However, with a focus on audience and purpose, and a well-organized introduction, body, and conclusion, an appropriate and effective presentation can be planned. By considering these concerns and the options available, a presentation can be a very effective means of communicating ideas in a professional setting.

Advantages, Disadvantages, and Guidelines for Four Types of Oral Presentations

Type of Presentation	Advantages	Disadvantages	Guidelines
Impromtu	• Delivered in a relaxed, conversational manner	• May be disorganized because the speaker can't prepare in advance • May be rambling and unfocused	• Stop and think before speaking • Ask the audience questions to determine what they want you to speak about
Extemporaneous	• Prepared ahead of time • Delivered in a relaxed, conversational manner • Allows speaker to adjust the presentation in response to the audience's reactions • Takes less time to create than a scripted presentation	• Can run over the allotted time • May cause the speaker to leave out information	• Rehearse the presentation • Use visual aids to guide you as you give the presentation (these aids will also help the audience) • Explain new information or terminology • Define unfamiliar terminology • Use simple, not fancy, language • Prepare notes or an outline
Scripted	• Prepared ahead of time • Allows the speaker to deliver complete, accurate information • Helps the speaker stay within the time limit	• Often delivered in an unnatural, boring manner • Doesn't allow the speaker to adjust to the audience's reactions • Takes a long time to prepare	• Use when the audience expects precision • Use visual aids and examples • Explain new information or terminology • Define unfamiliar terminology • Use simple, not fancy, language
Memorized	• Prepared ahead of time • Allows the speaker to deliver complete, accurate information • Helps the speaker stay within the time limit	• Makes the speaker seem stiff and formal • Can be disorganized as the speaker may lose his or her place • Takes a long time to prepare	• When possible, select either the extemporaneous or scripted style instead of a memorized presentation

From *Technical Communication* by Brenda Sims. Copyright © 2015 by Kendall Hunt Publishing Company. Reprinted by permission.

Presentation Slides

Hard-to-Read Slide

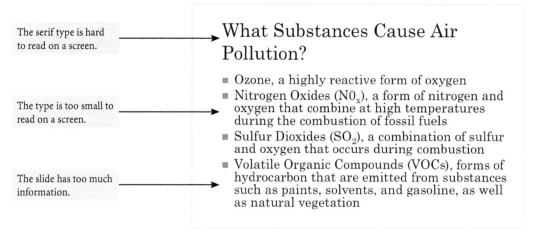

From *Technical Communication* by Brenda Sims. Copyright © 2015 by Kendall Hunt Publishing Company. Reprinted by permission.

Easy-to-Read Slide

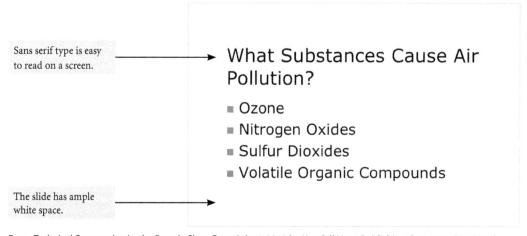

From *Technical Communication* by Brenda Sims. Copyright © 2015 by Kendall Hunt Publishing Company. Reprinted by permission.

Slide with a Distracting Background

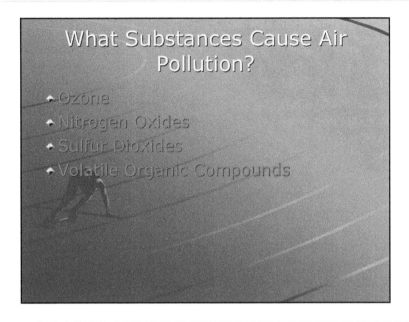

What Substances Cause Air Pollution?

- Ozone
- Nitrogen Oxides
- Sulfur Dioxides
- Volatile Organic Compounds

From *Technical Communication* by Brenda Sims. Copyright © 2015 by Kendall Hunt Publishing Company. Reprinted by permission.

TIPS for helping the audience enjoy your presentation

- **Talk slowly and distinctly.** Make sure the audience can understand your words.
- **Look the audience in the eye.** Audiences tend to be suspicious of speakers who don't maintain eye contact.
- **Speak with enthusiasm and confidence.** The audience doesn't want to listen to someone who seems uninterested or who lacks confidence.
- **Avoid verbal pauses (um, ah, uh, you know).** Rehearsing will help you eliminate them.
- **Don't read the slides.** When you read the slides, you are not maintaining eye contact or interacting with the audience.
- **Before you go on stage or to the podium, introduce yourself to some audience members.** Shake hands or make casual conversation.

From *Technical Communication* by Brenda Sims. Copyright © 2015 by Kendall Hunt Publishing Company. Reprinted by permission.

Taking it to the Workplace

Taking Cues from the Audience

Your audience will give you cues if you are not meeting their expectations. Karl Walinskas, author of *Reading Your Audience* (2001), suggests you take in those cues and adjust your delivery. He identifies three cues the audience will give you:

- **"The eyes have it."** Your first clue to audience interest is the eyes of each person. (If the room and the audience are large, observe the people in the first few rows.) Walinskas (2001, p. 24) suggests making sure "their eyes are *open!* ... Shut eyelids mean a bored crowd." Is the audience looking around the room or at their laps rather than at you and your visual aids? If so, change your pace or volume.
- **"Actions speak louder than words."** The audience's body language will give you cues. For example, if people in the audience are leaning back in their chairs getting comfortable (perhaps for a nap), change the pace of your presentation or get the audience involved. You might ask them to look at something on the screen or in a handout.
- **"The engagement factor."** Walinskas (2001, p. 24) explains that "the level to which your audience participates is a critical factor in determining how well they are receiving" your presentation. For example, even if you have asked them to hold questions until the end, someone in the audience may be so engaged that he or she can't wait. This signal tells you and the rest of the audience that your presentation is engaging.

The table that follows summarizes audience cues and suggests ways to adjust your presentation based on those cues.

Audience Cue	What It Means	How to Adjust
Shut eyelids	Boredom, fatigue	Change pace, volume, and subject matter; try humor to get them laughing and engaged
Wandering eyes	Distraction	Call attention to an important point and ask for the audience to focus; use humor
Mass exodus	Boredom; they've heard it before	Change tactics; add controversy; move on to the next point
Leaning back in seats	Apathy; waiting for something better	Try audience interaction; use humor
Shaking heads	Disagreement	Confront a head-shaker ("You disagree? Tell us why."); offer an alternative viewpoint that others embrace (even though you may not)
No questions during question and answer	Disinterest, confusion, hesitation	Plant seed questions with several people in the audience ahead of time to get the ball rolling; call on people whom you read as being most engaged during the presentation

Compiled from information retrieved 2008 from www.speakingconnection.com.

Taking it to the Workplace *continued*

Assignment

- Attend an oral presentation and evaluate how well the speaker delivers the presentation based on audience cues.
- Write a trip report to your instructor including the name of the speaker, the title, the date of the presentation, and your evaluation. For information on trip reports, see Chapter 14.

CHAPTER 6

Instructions

Instructions

One of the most common forms of communication within a workplace is creating instructions. Many positions in all industries find some on the job instructing that must be accomplished, whether you are training for the use of new equipment or services or showing a new employee routine practices that must be completed, you are creating and/or giving instructions. As consumers of products, we often find poorly written instructions on use or creation of an item and the common tendency is to ignore them. As writers in the workplace, this is an all too common situation: create instructions or manuals for a new product/service or training a new employee within a company. Writers often find themselves updating employees on routine practices as well. This can ensure that all employees are completing a process in the same manner every time it needs to be done.

Instructions are quite a complex process as you need to consider the audience and purpose, look to document design for ease of use and be certain that all information is present and communicated as clearly as possible using a clear introduction, body and conclusion. The bulk of the information will be communicated using lists and graphics throughout the document. It is very common to find safety concerns and mechanism descriptions with the instructions. The writer bears the tasks of communicating this information correctly and clearly to the reader in all cases.

Users' Questions about the Conventional Sections of Instructions

Conventional Sections	User's Questions
Introduction	• What is the purpose of the instructions? • What, if anything, should I know before beginning the task or using the equipment? • What materials and equipment do I need? • Is the equipment or the task safe? What do I need to do to protect the equipment or my surroundings from damage? What do I need to do to protect myself and others from injury? • How is the manual organized? If I am familiar with the tasks or equipment, where do I begin using the instructions? • What typographical conventions or terminology, if any, do I need to understand the instructions?
Step-by-step directions	• What do I do first? • What are the specific steps for performing the task? • Can I perform the task in more than one way?
Troubleshooting	• How do I solve problem X? What do I do if X happens? • Where can I get additional information if I cannot solve problem X?

From *Technical Communication* by Brenda Sims. Copyright © 2015 by Kendall Hunt Publishing Company. Reprinted by permission.

Effectively Designed Instructions

The writer uses task-oriented headings with verbs to focus on the action.

➤ Change the look of a bullet or number

1. To make changes to the bullets or numbers in your slides, on the **Home tab**, in the **Paragraph** group, click the arrow on either the **Bullets** or **Numbering** button, and then click **Bullets and Numbering.**

2. In the **Bullets and Numbering** dialog box, do one or more of the following:

   • To change the style of the bullets or numbering, on the **Bulleted** tab or the **Numbered** tab, click the style that you want.

   • To use a picture as a bullet, on the **Bulleted** tab, click **Picture**, and then scroll to find a picture icon that you want to use.

   • To add a character from the symbol list to the **Bulleted** or **Numbered** tabs, on the **Bulleted** tab, click **Customize**, click a symbol, and then click **OK**. You can apply the symbol to your slides from the style lists.

   • To change the color of the bullets or numbers, on the **Bulleted** tab or the **Numbered** tab, click **Color**, and then select a color.

   • To change the size of a bullet or number so that it is a specific size in relation to your text, on the **Bulleted** tab or the **Numbered** tab, click **Size**, and then enter a percentage.

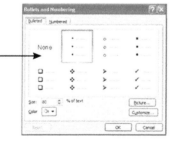

   • To convert the existing bulleted or numbered list to a **SmartArt graphic**, on the **Home tab**, in the **Paragraph** group, click **Convert to SmartArt Graphic.**

A copy of the screen helps users follow the directions.

Effectively Designed Instructions *continued*

The writer uses typeface, type size, and color consistently for the headings.

Change list levels (indent), spacing between text and points, and more

1. To create an indented (subordinate) list within a list, place the cursor at the start of the line that you want to indent, and then on the **Home tab**, in the Paragraph group, click Increase List Level.

The writer uses redlines and callout numbers to highlight information.

   1. Decrease List Level (indent)
   2. Increase List Level (indent)

2. To move text back to a less indented level in the list, place the cursor at the start of the line, and then on the **Home tab**, in the **Paragraph** group, click **Decrease List Level**.

3. To increase or decrease the space between a bullet or number and the text in a line, place the cursor at the start of the line of text. To view the ruler, on the **View** tab, in the **Show/Hide** group, click the **Ruler** check box. On the ruler, click the hanging indent (as shown in diagram below) and drag to space the text from the bullet or number.

Source: Retrieved from http://office.microsoft.com/enus/powerpoint/HA102580101033.aspx?mode-print

From *Technical Communication* by Brenda Sims. Copyright © 2015 by Kendall Hunt Publishing Company. Reprinted by permission.

Terms Used for Safety Alerts

Signal Word	Meaning	Example Graphic	Example Language
Danger	Alerts users to an immediate and serious hazardous situation, which will cause death or serious injury.	⚠DANGER	Danger: Moving parts can crush and cut.
Warning	Alerts users to a potentially hazardous situation, which may cause death or serious injury.	⚠WARNING	Warning: To reduce risk of electric shock, do not use this equipment near water.
Caution	Alerts users to the potential of a hazardous situation, which may cause minor or moderate injury.	⚠CAUTION	Caution: Do not use to exhaust hazardous materials and vapors.
Note	Gives users a tip or suggestion to help them complete a task or use equipment successfully.	NOTICE	Note: Turn off the mixer before scraping the bowl.

From *Technical Communication* by Brenda Sims. Copyright © 2015 by Kendall Hunt Publishing Company. Reprinted by permission.

Identifying Equipment Features

The writer uses a small page size to allow the manual to fit inside the cell phone box. Even though the page is small, it is uncluttered and easy to read.

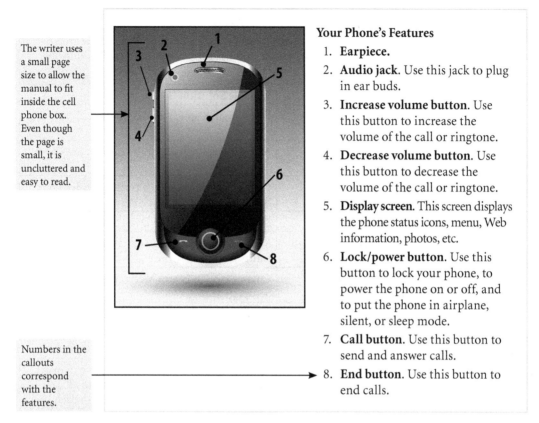

Your Phone's Features

1. **Earpiece.**
2. **Audio jack.** Use this jack to plug in ear buds.
3. **Increase volume button.** Use this button to increase the volume of the call or ringtone.
4. **Decrease volume button.** Use this button to decrease the volume of the call or ringtone.
5. **Display screen.** This screen displays the phone status icons, menu, Web information, photos, etc.
6. **Lock/power button.** Use this button to lock your phone, to power the phone on or off, and to put the phone in airplane, silent, or sleep mode.
7. **Call button.** Use this button to send and answer calls.
8. **End button.** Use this button to end calls.

Numbers in the callouts correspond with the features.

Source: Image © Pixachi, 2012. Used under license from Shutterstock, Inc.

From *Technical Communication* by Brenda Sims. Copyright © 2015 by Kendall Hunt Publishing Company. Reprinted by permission.

Frequently instructions may need to include a mechanism description. This information can be included in the Introduction section of the instructions. A mechanism description is a graphic of a product with all of the parts or functions clearly identified and labeled. This will help the reader to understand the functions and use of a given product or to service a product in some way. The graphic chosen for this portion needs to be clear and easy to read so that the functions can easily be identified by the reader.

Troubleshooting Guide

Troubleshooting Guidelines	
In the event that something is not working correctly on the oven, the display will show an error message that suggest that you call for service. Before calling for service, reference the following table for problems that you may be able to fix yourself.	
Problem	**Possible Solution (s)**
Displays and indicator lights are not working	Check that oven is receiving power.
Cook Navigator Screen is too dark or light	Adjust the brightness of the display. See Oven Setup, page 10.
Sounds are not working	Check that the volume is turned on. See Oven Setup, page 20.
Oven sounds are too loud or soft	Adjust the volume. See Oven Setup, page 20.
Menus are in the wrong language	Make sure tdesired language is selected. See Oven Setup, page 20.
Units and Measuremnets are displayed in metric and I want standard or vice versa	Change the Units and Measurements. See Oven Setup, page 20.
I forgot to save any changes to a recipe recently cooked	See Cooking a Recently Coooked Dish, page 7, Select "Save as Favorites."
Clock is set at the wrong time	Use the Set Timer Knob to reset. See page 6.
Oven light bulb is burned out	Call Customer Service at 866.44serve to order a replacement bulb. Instructions and all necessary components included with each bulb.
Oven Timer does not count down	Make sure the Set Timer Knob is pressed back into its origional position.
I experienced interference with my wireless phone	900MHz cordless phones are recommended to limit interference. Also try operating the wireless network on channel 1 if possible.

Source: *TurboChef 30″ Double Wall Speedcook Oven Use and Care Guide.* p. 37. Used with permission of TurboChef.

Taking it to the Workplace

Liability and Safety Information—Could You or Your Company Be Liable?

Are companies liable for damages when instructions for their products are imprecise or inaccurate? In *Martin v. Hacker*, the New York Court of Appeals unanimously decided that companies indeed are liable. This decision is especially interesting to people who write instructions because the court carefully analyzed the language of the instructions in a lawsuit over a drug-induced suicide. Eugene Martin was taking hydrochlorothazide and resperpine for high blood pressure; although he "had no history of mental illness or depression, [he] shot and killed himself in a drug-induced despondency" (Caher, 1995, p. 6). His widow alleged that the warning supplied with the drugs was insufficient. The court stated that the case centered on the drug manufacturer's obligation to fully reveal the potential hazards of its products. Therefore, the court specifically examined the safety warnings' accuracy, clarity, and consistency. The court scrutinized specific language that the writers used. The court dismissed the lawsuit, stating that the warnings "contained language which, on its face, adequately warned against the precise risk" (Martin v. Hacker, 1993).

According to this case, courts will carefully analyze the specific language of technical documents and will hold companies liable for that language (Parson, 1992). Companies and their writers, then, must be diligent in writing instructions—especially in terms of accuracy, clarity, and consistency because the "stakes are substantial" (Caher, 1995, p. 10). When a writer's work is unclear and a user "inadvertently reformats a hard drive, that's unfortunate"; but if a writer's inaccurate or unclear language claims a life, that's another matter altogether" (Caher, 1995, p. 10).

Assignment

1. Locate a similar case where a consumer sued an organization for damages based on presumably faulty instructions and safety information.
2. Summarize the case and be prepared to discuss it with your classmates.

From *Technical Communication* by Brenda Sims. Copyright © 2015 by Kendall Hunt Publishing Company. Reprinted by permission.

CHAPTER 7

Employment Communication

It is understood that in order to utilize the workplace skills discussed throughout a course on technical communications, one must first obtain a job or career. To promote success in doing so, several aspects of a job search become vital. Compiling a portfolio, composing an effective resume and cover letter, and preparing for a job interview are all daunting tasks that many find intimidating.

While experiences may vary based on region, field or industry, and company culture, there are still many ways to prepare for the job hunt and all that it entails. To ensure that you do not miss an opportunity, it is important to maintain a current and comprehensive portfolio and resume. As with any report, the formatting and design of the resume and cover letter may prove as important as their content, and just like a presentation, preparing for and communicating with your audience during a job interview is always a priority. By reviewing examples, planning ahead, and revising to ensure effectiveness, the job hunt can change from a daunting endeavor to a great opportunity for success.

We all know that the job market, like a workplace environment, is constantly changing and evolving to meet society's needs. That is why it is important to maintain a current resume, to understand modern job interview questions and practices, and to keep an updated portfolio. In addition, simply demonstrating that you prioritize these aspects of how you represent yourself to a potential employer can send a very positive message.

The Stages of Effective Job Search

Create Your Professional Brand
- Determine what employers want
- Build your brand
- Present your brand using your personal website, social media, business cards, and elevator pitches

Plan Your Job Search
- Contact your university placement center
- Respond to job postings on an organization's website
- Use an online job board
- Use your personal network, including LinkedIn

Write Your Résumé and Letter of Application
- Use a chronological or skills-based résumé format
- Prepare a plain-text résumé
- Include information in the letter that expands on the résumé

Prepare for a Successful Interview
- Do your homework before the interview
- Anticipate questions and prepare answers

Follow-up After the Interview
- Send a follow-up letter or email after the interview
- Send a follow-up letter or email when you receive a job offer
- Send a follow-up letter or email when you reject a job offer

From *Technical Communication* by Brenda Sims. Copyright © 2015 by Kendall Hunt Publishing Company. Reprinted by permission.

Case Study Analysis

Will Your Social Networking Sabotage Your Job Search?

Background

Millions of us log on to the Internet each day to network with friends and families through social networking sites such as Facebook. But, could you pay a price for the information or the lack of information on your social networking profiles?

Many job seekers have discovered that putting the details of their lives on social media sites has a downside. Job seekers aren't alone in paying a price for information on their social media sites. In March 2009, Dan Leone, a longtime employee and fan of the Philadelphia Eagles football organization, was fired over a Facebook posting. In the posting, he criticized the team for not resigning a player. Even though Leone had a long history of employment with the Philadelphia Eagles, his post got him fired (ESPN, 2009). You may think that the decision to fire a long-time employee was harsh; however, the Philadelphia Eagles aren't alone in scanning social media sites to monitor employees' posts and to act on negative postings. Employers also review the postings of potential employees for clues to behavior, maturity, abilities, etc.

As you review your social networking profile, follow these guidelines adapted from Metro Creative Communications (2009):

- **Use the "grandmother rule."** If the information or photograph you want to post is something that your grandmother would disapprove of, then most likely a job recruiter would frown on it—so don't post it.
- **Promote yourself.** Your social networking profile can benefit your job search. Post images of yourself doing positive activities such as volunteer work.
- **Don't "mug" for the cameras.** Images of you can appear on other people's profiles. Ask your friends and family to limit photo postings of you on their profiles. Remember that someone can snap a picture of you at any time.
- **Keep your opinions to yourself.** You may feel that recruiters and hiring managers do not have the right to use social networking sites to determine the worthiness of a prospective employee. Nonetheless, successful job seekers understand how recruiters and hiring managers use social networking, and those job seekers adjust their online profiles to avoid controversial topics. Regardless of how strongly you feel about politics, religion, or any other topic that might invite controversy, keep those opinions off your social networking profiles.

Assignment

1. Evaluate your social networking profiles on all platforms you use.
2. Write an informal memo to your instructor about your profile. Your memo should answer these questions:
   a. What information on the profile might cause hiring managers and recruiters to reject you?
   b. What information on the profile might encourage hiring managers and recruiters to hire you?
   c. What can you do to improve your social networking profiles?

Excerpts from a Professional's LinkedIn Profile

This excerpt from Katie Wilson's LinkedIn profile demonstrates that she is a highly motivated, talented professional who continues to update her skills.

Katie's photo shows that she is pleasant, professional, and approachable.

Her summary includes information on her primary roles and tasks in her jobs and her education. The summary demonstrates that she has varied skills and experiences that qualify her for a variety of jobs.

Katie Wilson

1st

Always be learning

Greater Philadelphia Area | Information Technology and Services

Current	CLONE SYSTEMS, INC.
Previous	Oracle, Department of Institutional Research and Effectiveness (IRE) (UNT)
Education	Drexel University

Send a message ▼

326
connections

Background

 Summary

At Clone Systems, I was responsible for implementing the entire marketing strategy. I reported directly to the CEO on progress I had made and provided analytics about strengths and weaknesses as each objective was achieved. I worked with developers to understand the intricacies of our products. I also collaborated with designers and sales to discover the best way to communicate to customers and prospects. Through these processes, I created visual and informative media to both gather data about customers and prospects to improve Clone's services and to ensure we were communicating effectively with all stakeholders.

As a technical writer, I focused constantly on improving the user experience. I focused mostly on the administrators' perspective, which forced me to think critically about the types of documentation an experienced user needs over a novice user. I worked diligently to design, format, and arrange the content to be as user friendly as possible.

My MBA program at Drexel University taught me about working with different businesses. I gained a breadth of knowledge on strategy, finance, and management. My week-long international residency in Vietnam also taught me about emerging markets and the challenges the global market faces. During this program, I analyzed market conditions and evaluated trends; made conclusions on how businesses were doing based on their financial records; and researched what businesses could do to improve.

Excerpts from a Professional's LinkedIn Profile
continued

Katie's experience section includes the logos of the companies where she has worked. It also uses verb phrases to demonstrate her work in her current and previous jobs. By listing both jobs, she shows that she is progressing in her skills, having moved from a position as a technical writer to a marketing director. She includes keywords to help potential employers locate her profile.

 Experience

Marketing Director
CLONE SYSTEMS, INC.

Clone Systems

July 2014 – Present (1 year) | Greater Philadelphia Area

Implemented marketing strategy, which included re-branding, updating messaging and making it consistent, attending and presenting at events, and developing new partnerships.

Developed product marketing content including data sheets, white papers, presentations, competitive analysis, newsletter, blogs, and demos to support sales in communicating with customers.

Updated CRM process to gather analytics on current customers. Gathered data on how often customers called for tech support, how customers responded to direct marketing campaigns, and what products and services most customers utilized. Turned this data into updated and measurable goals and objectives.

Researched potential prospects and partners and developed SWOT analysis to decide how best to interact through direct marketing, events, and referrals.

Worked with consultants to ensure content was optimized for SEO and ensured prospects, customers, and partners could find the info they needed when they needed it.

Technical Writer
Oracle

ORACLE

January 2010 – July 2014 (4 years 7 months)

Created and lead Advanced Documentation and Design team to improve designs, implement better user experiences, and discover advanced ways to deliver documentation for our products.

Collaborated with Functional Designers to develop products that met evolving customer needs.

Read product specs, recommended improvements, and utilized customer feedback to ensure customers had an advocate.

Separated 600 page admin doc into mini user-oriented books (so users could utilize only the books they needed) and turned them into HTML using Author-It.

Installed products to document the user process correctly and recommended ways to improve the installation process.

Monitored interns and new hires including training them to use our software and giving them tasks to document our products.

Excerpts from a Professional's LinkedIn Profile

continued

Katie's experience section includes the logos of the companies where she has worked. It also uses verb phrases to demonstrate her work in her current and previous jobs. By listing both jobs, she shows that she is progressing in her skills, having moved from a position as a technical writer to a marketing director. She includes keywords to help potential employers locate her profile.

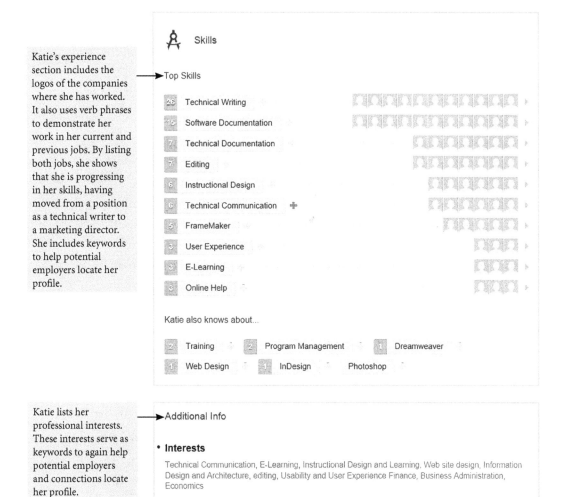

Skills

Top Skills

28	Technical Writing	
15	Software Documentation	
7	Technical Documentation	
7	Editing	
6	Instructional Design	
6	Technical Communication	
5	FrameMaker	
3	User Experience	
3	E-Learning	
3	Online Help	

Katie also knows about...

2 Training	2 Program Management	1 Dreamweaver
1 Web Design	1 InDesign	Photoshop

Katie lists her professional interests. These interests serve as keywords to again help potential employers and connections locate her profile.

Additional Info

- **Interests**

  Technical Communication, E-Learning, Instructional Design and Learning, Web site design, Information Design and Architecture, editing, Usability and User Experience Finance, Business Administration, Economics

Résumé Illustrating the Chronological and Skills-Based Organizations

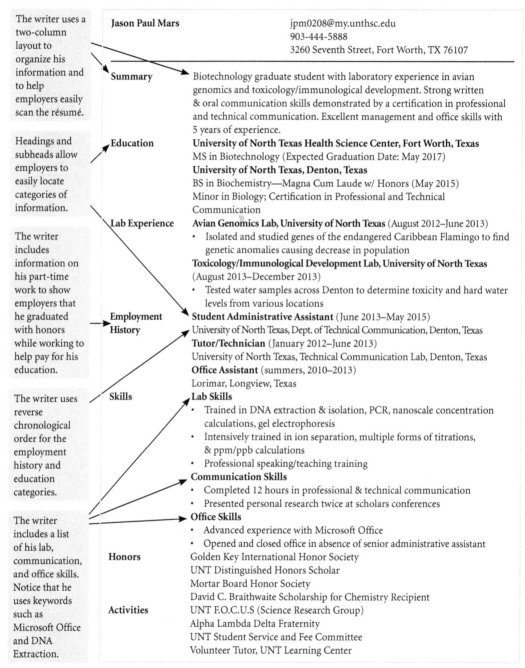

The writer uses a two-column layout to organize his information and to help employers easily scan the résumé.

Headings and subheads allow employers to easily locate categories of information.

The writer includes information on his part-time work to show employers that he graduated with honors while working to help pay for his education.

The writer uses reverse chronological order for the employment history and education categories.

The writer includes a list of his lab, communication, and office skills. Notice that he uses keywords such as Microsoft Office and DNA Extraction.

Jason Paul Mars

jpm0208@my.unthsc.edu
903-444-5888
3260 Seventh Street, Fort Worth, TX 76107

Summary

Biotechnology graduate student with laboratory experience in avian genomics and toxicology/immunological development. Strong written & oral communication skills demonstrated by a certification in professional and technical communication. Excellent management and office skills with 5 years of experience.

Education

University of North Texas Health Science Center, Fort Worth, Texas
MS in Biotechnology (Expected Graduation Date: May 2017)
University of North Texas, Denton, Texas
BS in Biochemistry—Magna Cum Laude w/ Honors (May 2015)
Minor in Biology; Certification in Professional and Technical Communication

Lab Experience

Avian Genomics Lab, University of North Texas (August 2012–June 2013)
• Isolated and studied genes of the endangered Caribbean Flamingo to find genetic anomalies causing decrease in population
Toxicology/Immunological Development Lab, University of North Texas (August 2013–December 2013)
• Tested water samples across Denton to determine toxicity and hard water levels from various locations

Employment History

Student Administrative Assistant (June 2013–May 2015)
University of North Texas, Dept. of Technical Communication, Denton, Texas
Tutor/Technician (January 2012–June 2013)
University of North Texas, Technical Communication Lab, Denton, Texas
Office Assistant (summers, 2010–2013)
Lorimar, Longview, Texas

Skills

Lab Skills
• Trained in DNA extraction & isolation, PCR, nanoscale concentration calculations, gel electrophoresis
• Intensively trained in ion separation, multiple forms of titrations, & ppm/ppb calculations
• Professional speaking/teaching training
Communication Skills
• Completed 12 hours in professional & technical communication
• Presented personal research twice at scholars conferences
Office Skills
• Advanced experience with Microsoft Office
• Opened and closed office in absence of senior administrative assistant

Honors

Golden Key International Honor Society
UNT Distinguished Honors Scholar
Mortar Board Honor Society
David C. Braithwaite Scholarship for Chemistry Recipient

Activities

UNT F.O.C.U.S (Science Research Group)
Alpha Lambda Delta Fraternity
UNT Student Service and Fee Committee
Volunteer Tutor, UNT Learning Center

Education Section of a Résumé

Education	**University of New Mexico**, Albuqerque, New Mexico B.S. in Mechanical Engineering Expected graduation in August 2016 GPA: 3.7/4.0 *Honors* Dean's List (Fall 2013, Spring 2014, Fall 2014, Spring 2015) Alpha Lambda Delta (Freshman Honor Society) Tau Beta Pi (General Engineering Society) The National Society of Collegiate Scholars Worked part-time to finance my education

From *Technical Communication* by Brenda Sims. Copyright © 2015 by Kendall Hunt Publishing Company. Reprinted by permission.

Employment History for a Job Seeker with Experience

Employment	**Texas Instruments, Inc.,** Dallas, Texas (2000–present) *Manufacturing Facilitator* (2005–present) • Facilitated two self-directed work teams of 26 team members performing screen printing and printing operations • Led screen printing team to win Gold Teaming for Excellence Award • Converted coating system to low VOC formulations that comply with existing air-quality standards *Reengineering Team Leader* (2002–2005) • Reengineered screen printing work flow to eliminate non-value-added effort and reduce task handoffs from one person to another • Reduced cycle time from 5 days to 2 days, increased productivity by 25%, and saved $250,000 annually • Received two Site Quality Improvement Award for reducing cycle time and improving quality (2003, 2004) *Process Improvement Engineer of Finish and Assembly Areas* (2000–2002) • Designed and installed custom equipment and machine upgrades that reduced manual labor required, saving $100,000 annually • Improved part racking on plating line, reducing scrap, saving $20,000 annually

From *Technical Communication* by Brenda Sims. Copyright © 2015 by Kendall Hunt Publishing Company. Reprinted by permission.

Employment History for a Job Seeker without Experience

Employment History	University of Washington, Seattle, Washington
	Lab Manager, Computer Labs (2013 to present)
	• Received Tutor of the Semester Award (Fall and Spring 2014)
	• Promoted to lab manager
	• Trained new tutors on how to use the software
	• Answered students' questions about Microsoft Word, Dreamweaver, InDesign, and Adobe Illustrator
	• Helped students and faculty with computer and software problems
	Chili's Lewisville, Texas
	Server (2011–2013)
	• Received the Outstanding Service Award (2012)

From *Technical Communication* by Brenda Sims. Copyright © 2015 by Kendall Hunt Publishing Company. Reprinted by permission.

Use Dynamic, Persuasive Language That Demonstrates What You Can Do

The guideline for word choice in your résumé is simple: Keep your writing style clear and uncluttered. Exclude extraneous information. Use dynamic, persuasive language (see Tips for Using Dynamic, Persuasive Language in a Résumé on the next page). The language in your résumé allows employers to create an impression of you. You want that impression to be positive.

The following examples illustrate phrases that use dynamic, persuasive language (the dynamic action verbs appear in bold type):

Not Dynamic/Persuasive	Created a computer program for students logging into the lab
Dynamic/Persuasive	Designed and programmed software that reduced the number of employees needed in the student computer labs and saved the university $16,640 annually
Not Dynamic/Persuasive	In charge of charity gala for my sorority
Dynamic/Persuasive	Coordinated the Red Dress charity gala that raised $8,600 for the American Heart Association
Not Dynamic/Persuasive	Was responsible for designing and installing custom equipment and upgrading machines
Dynamic/Persuasive	Designed and installed custom equipment and machine upgrades that reduced the manual labor required by $100,000 annually

From *Technical Communication* by Brenda Sims. Copyright © 2015 by Kendall Hunt Publishing Company. Reprinted by permission.

TIPS for Designing an Effective Résumé

- **Use headings and subheads to create visual categories.** Use type size to differentiate among the headings, subheads, and text. If you want to further differentiate headings and subheads from the text, use bold type.
- **Surround the headings with enough white space for employers to easily see them.** Highlight headings with white space (see Chapter 10 for information on white space).
- **Help employers locate information by using bulleted lists instead of paragraphs, especially in the employment history section.** An employer glancing at a paragraph might miss important information, such as an award received for excellence. A bulleted list highlights the award.
- **Use a clean, readable font.** Traditionally, Times New Roman was universally recommended for résumés. However, this recommendation is changing, in part, because résumés are often read on a screen rather than on paper. Fonts such as Times New Roman can be hard to read on a low-resolution screen, tablet, or smart phone. Many experts are now recommending clean sans serif fonts instead of Times New Roman. However, Nicole Fallen of Business News Daily (2015) writes "No matter which font family you choose, your résumé typeface should be easy on the eyes and show up well both in print and on a screen, regardless of size or formatting. It's also a good idea to choose a standard, universal font that works on any computer's operating system, as your résumé will also likely be scanned by automated applicant tracking software." Fallen recommends both serif and sans serif typefaces such as: Arial, Calibri, Garamond, Georgia, Times New Roman, and Trebuchet MS.
- **Use 8½ × 11-inch white bond paper.** Use good-quality paper. Because some employers will scan or copy your résumé, use white paper; even off-white paper will darken on a scanned image.
- **Proofread—then proofread again!** Ask another person to proofread your résumé. Make sure your résumé is free of grammatical, spelling, and punctuation errors. Even the smallest error can cost you an interview.

From *Technical Communication* by Brenda Sims. Copyright © 2015 by Kendall Hunt Publishing Company. Reprinted by permission.

Quadrant Test

Derek Hart
6494 W. Teton Blvd.
Las Vegas, NV 89129
(702) 365-2108
dhart@unlv.nevada.edu

A highly motivated student with strong communication skills, ability to multitask, stay organized and 3+ years of experience in the customer service industry.

EDUCATION

University of Nevada, Las Vegas   Expected: May 2015
Major: Finance
- GPA: 3.0

College of Southern Nevada   Associates Degree: May 2012
Major: Business
- GPA: 3.44

FINANCIAL SKILLS

Communication
- Prepared and delivered speeches for Oral Communications course
- Facilitated multiple group training sessions
- Communicated with employees and managers via e-mail daily

Multitasking/Organization
- Tasked with preparing and organizing multiple training sessions simultaneously
- Held multiple positions with multiple job functions

Data Skills
- Analyzed data to pitch buy/sell orders for Rebel Investment Group course
- Evaluated large sets of metrics data to determine areas for improvement

Computer
- Created income statements and balance sheets for Financial Accounting course
- Used Microsoft Excel at work and school
- Created fixed income spreadsheets for Investments course

WORK HISTORY

Apple Inc., Las Vegas, NV   2011 – Present
Specialist, Mentor, and In-Store Guest Trainer

The Betty R. and Robert S. Winthrop Foundation   2008 – Present
Board Treasurer

From *Business and Technical Writing* by Jeffrey Jablonski. Copyright © 2015 by Kendall Hunt Publishing Company. Reprinted by permission.

Vertical Columns Test

Virgil Perez

520 W. Island Crest Ave.
Las Vegas, NV 89129
(702) 624-9866
vperez@gmail.com

FINANCE SHARED SERVICES CENTER INTERN
Positioned to contribute accounting principles and auditing experience to MGM's diverse,
innovative environment for industry standard assurance, consistent and accurate
reporting, and company profit expansion

EDUCATION

University of Nevada, Las Vegas   Expected: May 2015
    BSBA in Accounting
    - GPA: 3.67
    - Dean's Honor List

WORK EXPERIENCE

Southwest Gas Corporation, Henderson, NV   Sept. 2013 – Present
    Gas Operations Business Safety Audit Intern
    - Convert to, update, and audit a new learning management system
    - Audit for safety certification compliance of employees and contractors
    - Present and maintain employee training module organization
    - Complete safety manual revisions for compliance

Acme Plumbing, Las Vegas, NV   May 2009 – Aug. 2013
    Bookkeeper/Office Assistant
    - Analyzed company accounting and financial data
    - Provided accounts receivable/payable, payroll, general accounting
    - Maintained accounting practices, procedures, and tax reporting
    - Provided customer service and technical problem solving

COMPUTER SKILLS

Quickbooks	Microsoft Excel	Microsoft PowerPoint
Sage (Peachtree)	Microsoft Word	Microsoft Access
Microsoft Publisher	Microsoft Outlook	AVS Video Editor

ACTIVITIES

Active Member, *Beta Alpha Psi*   Fall 2013-Present
    - Social Committee Membe   Spring 2014-Present
Active Member, Phi Kappa Phi Honor Society   Spring 2011-Present

Plain-Text Résumé

```
JASON PAUL MARS
jpm0208@my.unthsc.edu
903-444-5888
3260 Seventh Street, Fort Worth, TX 76107
***************************************************************************
SUMMARY
Biotechnology graduate student with laboratory experience in avian genomics and
toxicology/immunological development. Strong written & oral communication skills
demonstrated by a certification in professional and technical communication.
Excellent management and office skills with 5 years of experience.
***************************************************************************
EDUCATION
University of North Texas Health Science Center, Fort Worth, Texas
MS in Biotechnology (Expected Graduation Date: May 2017)

University of North Texas, Denton, Texas
BS in Biochemistry, Magna Cum Laude with Honors (May 2015)
Minor in Biology; Certification in Professional and Technical Communication
***************************************************************************
LAB EXPERIENCE
Avian Genomics Lab, University of North Texas (August 2012 - June 2013)
Isolated and studied genes of the endangered Caribbean Flamingo to find genetic
anomalies causing decrease in population.

Toxicology/Immunological Development Lab,
University of North Texas (August 2013 through December 2013)
Tested water samples across Denton to determine toxicity and hard water
Levels from various locations
***************************************************************************
EMPLOYMENT HISTORY
Student Administrative Assistant (June 2013 through May 2015)
University of North Texas, Dept. of Technical Communication, Denton, Texas
Tutor/Technician (January 2012 through 2013)
University of North Texas, Technical Communication Lab, Denton, Texas
Office Assistant
Lorimar, Longview, Texas (summers, 2010 through 2013)
***************************************************************************
SKILLS
Lab Skills
**Trained in DNA Extraction & Isolation, PCR, Nanoscale concentration calculations,
Gel electrophoresis
**Intensively trained in ion separation, multiple forms of titrations, & ppm/ppb
calculations
**Professional speaking/teaching training
Communication Skills
**Completed 12 hours in professional & technical communication
**Presented personal research twice at scholars conferences
Office Skills
**Advanced experience with Microsoft Office
**Opened and closed office in absence of senior administrative assistant
***************************************************************************
HONORS
Golden Key International Honor Society
UNT Distinguished Honors Scholar
Mortar Board Honor Society
David C. Braithwaite Scholarship for Chemistry Recipient
***************************************************************************
ACTIVITIES
UNT F.O.C.U.S (Science Research Group)
Alpha Lambda Delta Fraternity
UNT Student Service and Fee Committee
Volunteer Tutor, UNT Learning Center
```

TIPS for Formatting a Plain-Text Résumé

- **Use a line length of 65 or fewer characters.** Don't use word wrap when writing your résumé. Instead, use the space bar to create a new line after 65 or fewer characters.
- **Left justify the lines.** If you need to indent, use the spacebar, not the tab key. Tabs are lost when you convert the file to ASCII.
- **Use the asterisk, plus, and hyphen keys to mimic the effect of a bullet.** While you cannot use bullets, you can use the asterisk to give the effect of a bullet.
- **Break up blocks of text.** You can use all capital letters to indicate sections. For example, you might write EMPLOYMENT HISTORY or EDUCATION. You can also use a line of hyphens or asterisks to create a line to break up a block of text.
- **Use only the basic keyboard characters.** You can use the alphabet characters, the number and symbol keys, and the punctuation keys. Eliminate special formatting, symbols, and characters. When you convert a file to ASCII, formatting such as underlining, boldface, and italics are not recognized.

From *Technical Communication* by Brenda Sims. Copyright © 2015 by Kendall Hunt Publishing Company. Reprinted by permission.

Cover Letters
Introductory Paragraphs

Using a personal conact

Dr. Mathew Johnson suggested that I contact you about the project engineer position you currently have open in the Orlando office. My experience as an intern for Balfour Beatty provides me with the qualifications you are seeking. Would you please consider me for this position?

Using a job posting

My coursework in computer science and my experience as an intern for Microsoft qualify me for the Web designer position that you posted on CareerBuilders.com on May 16. Please consider me for this position.

Sending an unsolicited letter

My experience as an intern at BlueCross/Blue Shield, my work as a health technician at Parkland Hospital, and my degree in health management give me a solid foundation in health management. Please consider me for a position in your management training program.

From *Technical Communication* by Brenda Sims. Copyright © 2015 by Kendall Hunt Publishing Company. Reprinted by permission.

Experience and Education Paragraphs Written by a Job Seeker without Experience

> At Chambers University, I took many courses requiring writing. In an advanced technical communication course, I used InDesign to produce a 40-page user's manual for inventory software used by Minyards, Inc. (a regional grocery store chain). Currently, all Minyards stores use the manual to train new employees on the inventory system and as a reference guide for employees after initial training.
>
> For the past three years, I have worked in the Technical Communication Lab at Chambers University. I began as a lab tutor, assisting students with software questions, especially related to Microsoft Word, Adobe InDesign, and Microsoft PowerPoint. After 18 months, I was promoted to student lab manager. As manager, I work with the faculty to schedule lab classes, work with the lab tutors to set up their schedules, and conduct meetings each week with the tutors. Most recently, I set up a scheduling system that uses email instead of paper. This system saved $700 in annual paper costs. As manager and tutor in the lab, I have developed interpersonal skills that would benefit Writers, Inc.

Experience and Education Paragraphs Written by a Job Seeker with Experience

> While at Texas Instruments, I worked as an innovative design engineer. I have more than 15 years of research, production, and manufacturing experience, especially in the areas of machine design, power transmission, and structural analysis. I began as a process improvement engineer and was promoted to reengineering team leader and then to manufacturing facilitator. As manufacturing facilitator, I supervised two self-directed work teams of 26 team members. I led one of these teams, the screen printing team, to win the Gold Teaming for Excellence Award. I also received the Site Quality Improvement Award in 2013 and 2014 for increasing productivity by 25% annually.
>
> Along with my experience as a design engineer for Texas Instruments, I have a Bachelo's degree and a Master's degree in agricultural engineering from Texas A&M University. As part of my academic experience, I worked as a research assistant in the agricultural engineering department. I designed and constructed custom equipment and instrumentation used in energy conservation research.

Letter of Application Written by a Graduating Senior

204 Oak Street
Denton, TX 76205
August 6, 2015

Dr. Brandon McCarroll
Ericson Technology
2221 Lakeside Boulevard
Raleigh, NC 75082

Dear Dr. McCarroll:

The writer tells the employer where she found out about the job.

I am writing in response to your advertisement posted with University of North Texas career center. Would you please consider me for the entry-level position in technical documentation? I believe that my experience as an intern with AT&T, along with my education in technical communication and computer science from University of North Texas, qualify me for this position.

The writer identifies the position for which she is applying.

My education has given me a strong background in technical communication and computer science. I have concentrated on the design, programming, and documentation of web-based applications. For a senior-level course, with two students in computer science, I designed an intranet site for Texas Instruments. The site describes corporate history and culture at Texas Instruments. For my senior project, I designed a website for the dual degree program between a university in Toluca, Mexico and the University of North Texas. I conducted usability testing for this site. You may view the site at www.ltc.unt.edu/uaem.

The writer highlights and expands on information in her résumé.

While working as an intern for AT&T, I applied my classroom learning in a workplace environment. For one of my projects, I used my experience in designing online documents to develop a web-based application for wireless services offered by AT&T. More than 2,000 employees and customers use this application each week. During my second summer with AT&T, I updated this application. I also edited and proofread customer documentation for wireless service.

The writer refers to her résumé and tells the reader how to contact her.

My résumé provides further information about my education and work experience. Dr. McCarroll, I would enjoy the opportunity to meet with you to discuss my qualifications and résumé. You can reach me at (972) 555-5555 or at jdowdie@unt.edu.

The writer uses a professional email address.

Sincerely,

Jessie Dowdie

Jessie Dowdie

Enclosure

TIPS for a Successful Job Interview

Before the Interview

- **Do the research necessary to understand the position and the company with which you are interviewing.** Kip Hollister, founder and CEO of Hollister, Inc. staffing, explains that "one of the biggest turn-offs for a hiring manager is when an interviewing candidate has not done the research necessary to understand both the position and the company" (Hollister, in Zupek, 2007, p. 1). Find out what products the company produces or what services it provides. Visit the company's website; read its mission statement; find out about its locations, etc.

- **Create a list of solid questions to ask.** Near the end of the interview, the interviewer will probably ask you if you have questions. If you do not ask questions or if you do not ask good questions, the interviewer may assume you are uninterested in the position or that you are unprepared. Rachel Zupek of CareerBuilder. com recommends asking *open-ended questions*—questions that require more than a one- or two-word response. For example, ask, "How do you see me fitting in at your company?" or "What will make the person who takes this position successful?" (Zupek, 2007, p. 2).

- **Study lists of common interview questions.** Visit job boards and your college or university placement center for lists of common interview questions. These questions will help you prepare for what an interviewer may ask you.

- **Hold a mock interview.** Rehearse the interview by asking a friend, family member, or professor to hold a mock interview with you. Your college or university placement center may also conduct practice interviews.

- **Decide what you will wear.** Don't neglect your appearance. Bill Behn, a national director of staffing for Solomon Edwards Group, recommends that you "dress for the position you want to have" (Behn, in Zupek, 2007, p. 1). Dress conservatively; avoid clothing that is too revealing, too casual, or too outrageous. Don't wear too much jewelry or cologne, and don't chew gum.

- **Make sure you know where you are going for the interview.** If you will drive to the interview, make sure you know how to get there. If you are unfamiliar with the location, drive to the location a day or two before the interview so you are sure how to get there, where to park, and how long it will take to get there.

The Day of the Interview

- **Look over your list of questions.**
- **Arrive early.** If you arrive late, the interviewer may assume you have sloppy work habits.

At the Interview

- **Shake the interviewer's hand firmly and look him or her in the eyes.**
- **Use the interviewer's title, such as Mr., Dr., or Ms.** unless the interviewer says something like "Please call me Brenda."
- **Give more than yes or no responses to questions when appropriate.** Hollister says that interviewers want you to answer directly, but "it is OK to support your point with specific examples that are relevant to your work experience" (Hollister, in Zupek 2007, pp. 1–2). For example, if an interviewer asks if you had courses in technical communication, you might respond, "Yes, and in my technical communication class, I completed a volunteer's handbook for the local Boys & Girls Club."
- **Avoid speaking negatively about past employers** (Zupeck, 2007). If the interviewer asks you about a previous job, be prepared to show how you valued the experience. For example, say, "I learned how to solve problems" or "The job taught me how to work with people with various work styles."

Interview Questions

One of the steps to prepare for the interview is to anticipate any questions you may be asked. Interviewers are looking for what you have to say about your qualifications as well as how you conduct yourself during the interview. Preparing for these types of questions beforehand can provide you with the confidence you need.

There are some questions that are almost always asked, in any field by any potential employer. While these may sound easy at first, the pressure you feel in the moment and a desire to get them "right" may become an issue. Prepare your responses so that you are ready to answer quickly and with confidence. You don't need to memorize a "script", but have an outline of the key points you wish to address in mind. In your answers you should focus on your qualifications for the workplace. You do not want to provide personal information within the answers to these questions. To get started, consider your resume and the body paragraph(s) of your cover letter.

Frequently Asked Universal Questions:
1. Tell me a little bit about yourself.

   Answer: I am a hardworking and very driven individual that enjoys a challenge. I have several years of experience working in customer service through previous jobs and have learned how to resolve customer disputes effectively.
2. What makes you the right person for this job?
3. Why would you like to work *here*/for *us*?
4. Where do you see yourself in 5/10 years?

Some questions make you choose between two equally valuable answers. These "either/or" questions may not seem dangerous, but they contain a hidden peril—whatever you don't select may sound like a negative quality. For instance, if you answer question #1 with "I learned more at work," the interviewer(s) may infer you were a subpar student; if your answer to questions #2 is that you work better alone, their assumption may be that you don't get along well with others.

To avoid this, focus on the one you **don't** select. First and foremost, always answer **honestly**. Saying "I like both" is not the "right" answer, and it's simply not true—all humans have preferences. Your interviewer(s) asked, and they deserve an honest answer about you. So respond with your choice, but then develop your response based on the one you **didn't** pick. For instance, if as a response to question #1 you state "I learned more at work," then proceed to discuss how your academic career did also provide some benefit to your development, in a full, detailed answer.

<u>Either/Or Questions:</u>

1. What has prepared you more for this career: your work or academic experience(s)?

   Answer: I have found I learned more in my previous jobs than in my class-room experiences. The jobs offered me a place to practice actions and concepts while the classroom provided me a place to understand the concepts and what would be good responses to situations that might be presented to me as an employee.

2. Do you prefer to work alone or in a team dynamic?

It's easy to respond to questions that are positive in nature during an interview, in which we discuss our strengths as we "sell" ourselves. However, responding to "negative" questions can be much trickier. We don't want to say anything to defame ourselves, but the question was posed.

Again, first and foremost, be **honest**. Saying "I'm perfect", or the ever-popular "I'm such a perfectionist, my greatest weakness is how great I am" are not "correct" responses.

To respond effectively, choose a negative quality/issue/problem that you personally have and discuss in a detailed, specific response how you **overcame** that negative attribute. Tell the truth, but spin the negative question into a way to speak positively about yourself.

<u>Negative Questions:</u>

1. What is your greatest weakness?

   Answer: I have realized that I am a procrastinator. I would rather wait then jump into a project, however I had to overcome that feeling while attending college classes. While it was difficult, I learned to budget my time better and not push projects and papers off to the last minute. Doing a project in stages offered me a better solution and a better grade for my classwork.

2. Discuss an issue you had at your previous employer/in school.

3. What do/did you find most challenging in school? ...at your previously place of <u>employment</u>?

Interview Questions *continued*

Everyone likes to feel special, and this is true of your interviewers as well. You never want them to feel as if they are simply the third of your five interviews that day. A basic familiarity with the company/business is paramount for an effective job interview, and in this day and age five brief minutes on the internet can yield invaluable information regarding the nature and culture of the employer to which you are applying.

Be prepared through some fundamental research prior to the interview for questions that give you an opportunity to discuss their company, focusing upon how you would be a cohesive, beneficial addition to it.

Questions Specific to the Interviewer/Potential Employer:

1. Why would you like to work here/for us?

   Answer: I have found that your company strives to satisfy your patient's needs through excellent care. I want to be part of that caring service to all patients and provide them with the care and service they need to recuperate from whatever illness or injury they have.

2. How did you hear about this position?
3. What do you feel you can bring to our company/business?
4. Do you have any questions for us?

   You should also be prepared to ask question of the interviewers. There will be a time set aside for all interviewees to ask questions of the interviewers about the company/job. You want to concentrate on company visions and future plans. You can also ask questions about the job responsibilities for which you are interviewing.

Some questions are simply not legal to be asked in an interview situation. Unfortunately, that does not mean such things never occur. These overly-personal illegal questions focus on your personal beliefs, attributes or status that should not be fairly taken into consideration during the hiring process. Your preparation here will consist of how to handle yourself if you are faced with one of these types of questions. Remember to focus on work responsibilities and not to reveal the personal nature of the question.

Illegal Questions:

1. Are you married/single?

   Answer: My marital status will have no bearing on my work ethic or my responsibilities.

2. Do you plan to have children?
3. What church do you attend?
4. What is your ethnic background?

Interview Questions *continued*

Here is a list of generic questions that you can use to prepare for your next interview situation.

1. What are your strengths and weaknesses?
2. Why are you looking to change jobs?
3. How do you spend your spare time?
4. If I were to ask your boss to describe you, what would he/she say?
5. What is a difficult work environment for you?
6. What are you looking for in a job?
7. How did you find out about our company?
8. Where do you see yourself in 1 year? In 5 years?
9. Give me an example of a time when you took initiative to get things done.
10. What can you do for our company?
11. What was the last teamwork situation you were in that was difficult?
12. What new competencies or skills have you recently developed?
13. Have you participated in any volunteer or community work? What did you learn there?
14. How do you feel about routine work?
15. Why did you choose this career?
16. How do you define your personal work style?
17. What does great customer service mean to you?
18. What kind of boss would you like?
19. Tell me about the technology you currently use and what you feel your proficiency level is.
20. Do you have plans for additional training or education?
21. Do you feel you have good communication skills? Why?
22. What three things do you want me to know about you?
23. Why did you choose this career? Where will it lead you?
24. Do you handle conflict well?
25. Would you rather work with information or people? Why?
26. Tell me about the last time you made a mistake at work.
27. Tell me about a time when you had a problem with a coworker.
28. Are you a goal oriented person?
29. How has your education prepared you for your career?
30. Have you ever had a boss you didn't like, and what did you do about it?
31. What motivates you and how do you motivate people?

Post-Interview Follow-Up Letter

402 Spring Avenue, Apt. 6C
Alexandria, VA 23097
May 4, 2015

Mr. Dwight Wilson
Senior Production Engineer
I-2 Technology, Inc.
1111 Jorge Mendoza Blvd.
San Diego, CA 92093

Dear Mr. Wilson:

Thank you for taking time from your busy schedule yesterday to show me I-2 Technology's facilities and to discuss the quality control job. I especially enjoyed meeting many of your coworkers. Please thank Ms. Johnson in the quality control division for the tour she gave me of the facility.

As a result of our visit, I have a good understanding of I-2 Technology and appreciate its progressive approach to maximizing production without sacrificing quality control. I feel confident that my work as an intern at Boeing provides the experience you are looking for in your team.

I-2 Technology's place in the semiconductor industry and your colleagues in the quality control division confirm my impression that I-2 Technology would be an exciting place to work. If I can answer further questions, please call me at (703) 555-0922.

Best regards,

Cynthia Demsey

Cynthia Demsey

Career Portfolio

Vitals

File the completed form in the Personal section of your career portfolio

Complete name	
Date of Birth:	**Place of Birth (City, State, Country)**
Email:	**Telephone:**
If U.S. Citizen by Naturalization, complete the following:	
Alien Registration Number	Present Citizenship
Date of Entry	Port of Entry
Military Service (Past or Present)	
Branch/Rank	Dates (from-to)
Emergency Contacts: List two individuals who will be your contacts in the event you are involved in an emergency situation.	
1.	
2.	

Addresses

List all addresses you have used for the past 10 years. Record the oldest first and proceed to the present. File the completed form in the Personal section of the portfolio

Dates	Street/Mailing Address	City	State	Zip Code

Education Summary

List all schools attended in chronological order. **Begin with high school**. File the completed form in the Education section of the portfolio

Dates Attended	School Name	Mailing Address City, State, Zip	Major

Education Record

Complete one form for each school listed on the Education Summary. Attach copies of support documents: diploma, transcript, certificates, and awards. Include this form in the Education section of the portfolio.

Name of School or Organization		
Address		
Type of Degree/Program	**Date Earned**	**Grade Point Average**
Key Courses		
Awards/Achievements Earned		
Extracurricular Activities		

Employer Summary

List all jobs in chronological order. **Begin with the most recent.** File this form in the Employment section of the portfolio.

Dates Employed	Business Name Mailing Address	Job Title	Pay Rates

Include one form for every job listed. Include this form in the Employer section of the portfolio.

Employer Name				Avg Hrs Worked/Week
Hire Date	Beginning Wage	Beginning Job Title		Beginning Supervisor
Term. Date	Ending Wage	Ending Job Title		Ending Supervisor
Job Description				
Special Recognitions/Awards				
Licenses held because of job				
What I liked best about this job is/was….				
What I liked least about this job is/was….				

Licenses & Certifications

List all licenses and certificates you hold/held including a driver's license, CPR certification, first aid, etc. File the completed form in the Education section of the portfolio.

Type of License	Issuing Agent	License Number (if applicable)	Expiration Date

Other Activities Summary

Record all unpaid activities in chronological order. Use as many pages as necessary. Include relevant volunteer work, club memberships, home activities, hobbies, sports, special interests, etc. Include this form in the Activities section of the portfolio.

Dates	Name of Activity or Group City and State	Description of Activity or Involvement

Professional References

Reference #1

Name _____

Title/Position _____

Company/Business _____

Company/Business Address _____

_____

Phone _____

Email _____

Reference #2

Name _____

Title/Position _____

Company/Business _____

Company/Business Address _____

_____

Phone _____

Email _____

Reference #3

Name _____

Title/Position _____

Company/Business _____

Company/Business Address _____

_____

Phone _____

Email _____

CHAPTER 8

Technical Research

When people heard the term "research," many once thought that it would mean a trip to the local library to sift through card catalogues and bookshelves; to most contemporary students, "research" may now mean a quick Google search of a few key words. But conducting what is considered technical research is often a more interactive, less "academic" approach.

The goal of technical research is often quite clear: to get information and answer the questions necessary to achieve your *purpose*. But what this entails can vary greatly. Of course, the Internet offers us a treasure trove of information; however, much research may involve speaking to other people to obtain the information needed. This can include conducting interviews, creating questionnaires, or compiling surveys, all of which are commonly used methods of technical research.

As with any report or presentation, planning in advance is key to ensuring success in your research. While a variety of techniques may work in different situations, there are always key considerations of which you should be aware to promote the benefits of the research you conduct.

Bill's Research Plan

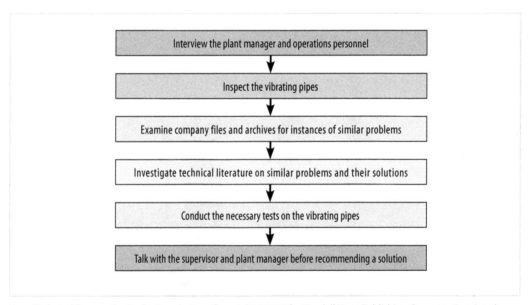

Planning Your Research

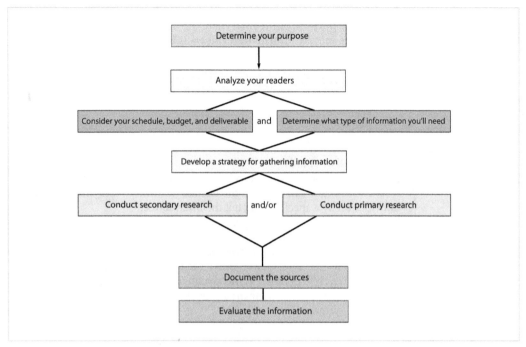

From *Technical Communication* by Brenda Sims. Copyright © 2015 by Kendall Hunt Publishing Company. Reprinted by permission.

TIPS for Effective Formal Interviews

Determine the purpose of the interview	**Before the interview** • **Identify the purpose of the interview.** • **Identify the specific information you want to gather.** Think about Bill's interview with Richard Hampton, operations manager at the plant. Bill might identify the purpose of this interview as follows: *The purpose of my interview with Richard Hampton is to identify the frequency of the vibration, its effect on the plant's operation, and which operations seem to trigger the vibration. I also want to know what he believes is causing the vibration.*
Contact the interviewee to set up the interview	**When you call or email** • **State the purpose of your interview,** so the interviewee can tell you whether he or she can give you the needed information. If you need the information by a specific date, tell the interviewee. • **Be flexible about the time.** If possible, let the interviewee determine the time and date for the interview. • **Hold the interview at the interviewee's office or at a location most convenient for the interviewee.** Make the interview location convenient for the interviewee even if it is inconvenient for you. • **Ask permission to record the interview** if you plan to use audio- or video-recording equipment. • **Offer to submit questions ahead of time.**

Prepare for the interview	**Before the interview**
	• **Find out as much about your subject and the interviewee as possible.**
	• **Plan your questions.**
	• **Gather background information.** Look at secondary sources. You look unprepared if you ask questions that the professional literature answers.
	• **Plan specific, open-ended questions.** Avoid questions that can be answered with yes/no.
	  • **Yes/no question:** *Can greenhouse emissions affect children's health?*
	  • **Open-ended question:** *How do greenhouse emissions affect children's health?*
	• **Avoid leading, biased questions.**
	  • **Leading/biased:** *Don't you agree that greenhouse emissions are one of the greatest dangers to children's health in large cities?*
	  • **Impartial:** *How do you see greenhouse emissions as affecting children's health in large cities?*
	• **Write each question on a separate notecard.** You can also put the questions on a file on your laptop or other electronic device. Be sure to use wide margins so you can see the questions and summarize the answers.

Prepare yourself	**Before the interview** • Give yourself plenty of time to arrive early for the interview. • Arrive on time (or a little early). • Check your video- and audio-recording equipment if you plan to use it.

TIPS for Effective Formal Interviews *continued*

Conduct the interview	**At the beginning of the interview**
	• Thank the interviewee for agreeing to do the interview.
	• State the purpose of the interview.
	• Tell the interviewee how you plan to use the information.
	• Respect cultural differences. Make sure you use the appropriate level of formality, politeness, and other behaviors in the given culture. (See Chapter 2.)
	
	During the interview
	• Let the interviewee do most of the talking.
	• Maintain eye contact. Your interviewee will give you more information if you show you are sincerely interested.
	• Use your prepared questions.
	• Ask follow-up questions, such as
	  • *Can you give me an example?*
	  • *What additional actions would you suggest?*
	• If you don't understand an answer, ask the interviewee clarifying questions, such as
	  • *Can you give an example?*
	  • *Can you simplify?*
	  • *Would you go over that again, please?*
	• Verbally summarize the interviewee's answers to make sure you understood.
	• If the interviewee gets off the subject, be prepared to respectfully move the interview back to the intended focus. You might say, *Thank you for that interesting information. I know our time is short, so let's move on to the next question.*
	• Take notes only as necessary. Write only the important information. Don't write so much that you can't maintain some eye contact with the interviewee or that the interviewee has to wait while you complete your notes.
	
	At the end of the interview
	• Ask the interviewee for final comments.
	  • *Would you like to add any other information?*
	  • *Can you suggest other sources or people whom I should interview?*
	• Ask permission to quote the interviewee (if you have not already done so).
	• Ask for the interviewee's correct title and position.
	• Ask if you may contact the interviewee again if you have questions or need to verify information.
	• Offer to send the interviewee a copy of your notes, so he or she can review the information for accuracy.
	• Thank the interviewee for his or her time.
	• Leave promptly.

Follow up	**After the interview** • Write down the information that you want to remember from the interview. • Write the interviewee a thank-you note within two or three days.

From *Technical Communication* by Brenda Sims. Copyright © 2015 by Kendall Hunt Publishing Company. Reprinted by permission.

Types of Questions Used in Questionnaires

Type of Question	Type of Answer	Example
Multiple choice	Respondents select from one or more alternatives	What is your classification? ____ Freshman ____ Junior ____ Sophomore ____ Senior ____ Graduate
Yes or no	Respondents select "yes" or "no"	Would you use the express rail service to commute to your office? ____ Yes ____ No
Likert scale	Respondents rank their answers on a scale. Select an even number of choices.	The online reporting system has made my job easier. Circle your response. Strongly disagree Disagree Agree Strongly agree
Semantic differential scale	Respondents rate their answers on a continuum of opposing concepts. Limit the choices to no fewer than 3 and no more than 11. Use this type of question to measure attitudes and feelings.	Your technical communication class is Easy _____ Hard Interesting _____ Boring Current _____ Out of date
Ranking	Respondents rank (prioritize) their answers.	Rank the importance of the following factors when you purchase a new car. Put a 1 next to the most important factor, a 2 next to the second most important factor, and so on. ____ Fuel economy ____ Safety ratings ____ Price ____ Consumer satisfaction ratings ____ Size ____ Dealership ____ Color ____ Upgrades available
Formal rating scale	Respondents rate an item or quality on a specific scale, usually 1 to 5 or 1 to 10.	How do you rate your satisfaction with your new vehicle? Please circle only one rating, with 1 being not satisfied and 5 being satisfied. 1 2 3 4 5 Not satisfied Satisfied
Checklists	Respondents check one answer. With an expanded checklist, respondents may check more than one response. (See the example to the right.) The list of responses should include any possible answer from the respondents and be mutually exclusive. The response of "other" allows for responses that you may not have considered; however, the varied answers will make coding your questionnaire more difficult.	Which of the following activities describes tasks you complete daily using a computer? (Check all that apply.) ____ Check and send email ____ Surf the Internet ____ Communicate through social media ____ Pay bills ____ Watch videos ____ Get directions ____ Get news and weather ____ Check my stocks ____ Use word processing software ____ Prepare spreadsheets ____ Other (please explain) _____
Short answer/essay	Respondents answer open-ended questions using phrases or sentences.	How well do you think telecommuting will work in your department? What do you believe are the advantages and disadvantages of telecommuting?

From *Technical Communication* by Brenda Sims. Copyright © 2015 by Kendall Hunt Publishing Company. Reprinted by permission.

MALL SHOPPERS SURVEY

1. How often do you shop here—daily, weekly, monthly, longer?
2. Did you have trouble parking? (NOTE: this is ambiguous and difficult to answer because how is *trouble* defined?) A better question might be—
   How long did it take to park—a minute, less than five minutes, more than five minutes?
3. Are you here today to—buy a household item, something for yourself, a gift, meet someone, window shop, or spend a few hours?
4. In which department store do you spend the most time?
5. In which specialty store do you spend the most time?
6. How much do you spend on an average visit to the mall—less than $50, less than $100, more than $100, more than $200, other?
7. What specialty stores would you like to see? _____
8. What improvements or additions would you like to see to the food court? _____
   _____
9. Demographic questions
10. Comment:

TOURIST SURVEY AND QUESTIONNAIRE
Adams Homestead—Quincy, Massachusetts

1. From which state are you visiting? _____
   If from Massachusetts, what town? _____
2. How long is your current trip? _____
3. How long did you spend at the Adams Homestead? _____
4. List other Massachusetts sites you plan to visit:
   _____
5. On a scale of 1–5, with 5 being the best, rate the following items:
   Courtesy of staff   1 2 3 4 5
   Professionalism   1 2 3 4 5
   Historical Information   1 2 3 4 5
6. Are children with you Y/N? How many? _____
7. Did you purchase items from the gift shop? What items? _____
8. Demographic questions: age, gender, marital status, income level, education level
9. Comments:

From *Technical Writing in the Workplace* by Harvey Ussach. Copyright © 2014 by Kendall Hunt Publishing Company. Reprinted by permission.

RESTAURANT SURVEY
(a national pancake chain)

My wife and I fill out a lot of these surveys. They start with an electronic cover letter stating that consumer feedback is important and that it should not take more than fifteen minutes. After typing in the store number, it offers English or Spanish options, then requests the time of day, the number of people in the party, how often we dine at the restaurant, and the following information:

1. If the welcome was pleasant
2. If the wait was long for service
3. If the table was clean
4. If the waitperson suggested a special promotion
5. If the meal arrived as ordered
6. If not, was the problem corrected satisfactorily
7. If the customer would recommend the restaurant to others
8. If the customer would return
9. Demographic questions
10. Comments

From *Technical Writing in the Workplace* by Harvey Ussach. Copyright © 2014 by Kendall Hunt Publishing Company. Reprinted by permission.

TIPS for Searching Online for Information

- **Use more than one search engine.** Search engines are not identical; they index only a portion of the information available online. Use more than one search engine to make sure you get the most reliable, up-to-date information. If you don't find the information you need or if you get limited results, try a different search engine.
- **Use varied keywords or search phrases.** For example, if you are looking for information on greenhouse gases, you might use the terms greenhouse gases, greenhouse effect, greenhouse gas emissions, global warming, or climate change. By using all these terms, you will gather more information.
- **Use discipline-specific websites when possible.** Once you find a list of links, select the websites that are discipline specific. Let's consider the greenhouse gas example. If you search for greenhouse gas emissions, you may find links to information from the U.S. Environmental Protection Agency (EPA), the U.S. Department of Energy (DOE), and Wikipedia. The specialized websites would be the EPA and DOE, not Wikipedia.
- **Download only what you need.** Many websites include graphics, video files, and sound. If you only need the text, download only that information. Graphics, video files, and sound take up valuable memory on your computer or flash drive.
- **Save or print what you need.** Note the URL or copy and paste it and the date you accessed the information. Keep an electronic file of the URLs where you have accessed information. You will appreciate this file when you prepare your works cited or list of references.
- **Consider the ethics of using information from the Internet.** Information, videos, sounds, and graphics that you download from the Internet may be the intellectual property of an author or company. The information may be copyrighted. Make sure you credit the source and/or get permission to use the information, video, sound, or graphic.

From *Technical Communication* by Brenda Sims. Copyright © 2015 by Kendall Hunt Publishing Company. Reprinted by permission.

Questions for Evaluating Online Sources

Is the Online Source . . .	Questions to Ask	Comments
Written or prepared by reliable authors?	• Who created the website or the information? • What are the credentials of the author(s)? • If you don't recognize the name of the author(s), company, or organization, did you find the site through another reliable source? • Does the site contain biographical information on the author(s)? • Can you find references to the author's, company's, or organization's credentials or work through other search engines or databases?	Anyone, whether qualified or not, can publish information online and all voices appear equal. • Be wary of using information from an author, company, or organization you don't recognize, or from a source that you cannot verify as credible. • If you cannot find who operates a website, find information from another source.
Published by a reliable group?	• Who is the website's publisher? • What makes the publisher qualified to produce the site? • Is the publisher affiliated with a reputable group or organization? • Does the domain name give you information about the publisher and its purpose? For example, epa.gov tells you that the publisher is a government institution. • Does the website include contact information for the publisher?	If the website is published from a personal account with an Internet service provider, the site may contain unreliable information. If the information looks interesting or valuable, verify that information through other sources. If you cannot verify it, don't use it.
Up-to-date?	• When was the website or document created or published? • When was the site or document updated or revised? Has it been updated in the last three months? • Are the links up-to-date? Do the links work? • Is the site "under construction" or only partially complete?	If the website has not been updated in the last three months, the information may not be up-to-date or reliable. If the site or item is "under construction," you may want to use another site or source. If the links don't work, the site may not contain up-to-date information.
Presented clearly and accurately?	• Is the site well constructed? Does it have a professional appearance and design? • Does the site follow basic rules of grammar, spelling, and punctuation? • Do the authors cite sources? Do they support all claims with appropriate evidence? • Does the information appear biased?	If a site looks unprofessional, its information may be unreliable. If the site doesn't follow the basic rules of grammar, spelling, and punctuation, the information may be unreliable or inaccurate. If the authors do not cite sources or support their claims, use other sources. A reliable site • has a professional, well-constructed design • follows the basic conventions of grammar, punctuation, and spelling • supports all claims • documents sources • presents unbiased information or tells you when authors are stating opinions

Taking it to the Workplace

Copyright Laws and Your Research

Passed by the U.S. Congress, the Copyright Act of 1976 and the Digital Millennium Copyright Act of 1998 protect the authors of published and unpublished works. Under U.S. law, the author of a work is entitled to the profits if someone sells or distributes the work, except in cases of "fair use." For example, the information on a website may be copyrighted: the text, artwork, music, photographs, and audiovisual materials (including sounds). You can use copyright-protected works without the author's permission if you follow the fair use guidelines established by the Copyright Act of 1976. This law protects you if you use a small portion of an author's work to benefit the public. Fair use allows you to use works for education, research, criticism, news reporting, and scholarship purposes that are nonprofit in nature. To determine fair use, consider these factors:

- **The purpose of the use.** Is the use for commercial, nonprofit, or educational purposes? If you are using the work for commercial purposes, you may be violating the copyright law. You are responsible for knowing if the work is copyrighted.
- **The nature and purpose of the copyrighted work.** If the information is essential for the good of the public, you may be able to use the copyrighted work without the author's permission.
- **The amount and substantiality of the portion of the work used.** The law doesn't give strict guidelines, so you must use your judgment to determine how much of a copyrighted work you can use without the author's permission. For example, if you use 400 words of a 1,000-word document, you are not following fair use guidelines. If you use 400 words of a 100,000-word document, you are following fair use guidelines. If you are using even a part of a copyrighted graphic, you must get permission. You can't use a portion of a copyrighted graphic.

- **The effect of the use on the potential market for or value of the copyrighted work.** If your use of the copyrighted document hurts the author's potential to profit from the work or hurts the potential value of the work, you have violated fair use guidelines.

Taking it to the Workplace *continued*

As you write and create documents—online or in print—ask yourself these questions:
- Have you relied on information from copyrighted works? If so, do you have permission from the author(s) to use the work?
- Have you appropriately cited sources or acknowledged that you have used the work by permission of the author?
- Are you unfairly profiting from the copyrighted work of the author(s)?
- Have you asked for legal advice? If you don't know whether you can legally use a portion of work, ask for advice from legal counsel. If you ask for advice, you may prevent legal action against you or your employer.
- Are you doing the right thing? (For more information on ethics and doing the right thing, see Chapter 4.)

Assignment

Visit these websites to learn more about U.S. copyright laws.
- U.S. Copyright Office: www.copyright.gov
- Copyright Clearance Center: www.copyright.com

After visiting these websites, write a memo to your instructor answering these questions:
- How do you know if a document is copyrighted?
- What is the Copyright Clearance Center? How can students and businesses use the center's website?
- How do you register a copyright?
- How long is a copyright protected?
- What works are protected by copyright?
- What is not protected by copyright?
- How does copyright affect you when conducting research?

From *Technical Communication* by Brenda Sims. Copyright © 2015 by Kendall Hunt Publishing Company. Reprinted by permission.

Annual Report Discussion

Using an annual report for a company you have chosen, prepare to speak to the class or write about the following items as listed in the Annual Report:

1. Why did you choose this company? What is your interest in this company? How did you find out about this company?

2. What is the company's major product or service? Who is the primary customer for this product/service?

3. Discuss the company's history. Include beginnings, major changes such as mergers, moves, etc.

4. Discuss the company's philosophy and values system. (this title will vary in Annual Reports) What is the belief system? What are employees encouraged to do?

5. How is the company governed or what is the management structure? Be sure to include names and positions.

6. What information is included about employment practices? Include items such as benefit packages, employee requirements such as education, experience levels, etc.

7. What is the company's presence in our local area? How many outlets? How are they located/owned? (chain, independently, etc)

CHAPTER 9

Proposals

Technical writers often have to create reports within the workplace in many areas. A common form of a report is a proposal. This report offers suggestions for an action such as a purchase of equipment or services or a change in a workplace such as a different login procedure that eliminates hacking of computer accounts. Proposals may be solicited, which means they may be requested by an audience. Proposals may be unsolicited, meaning the writer created this report without any prior request from an audience member. Proposals primarily are persuasive in nature as they are encouraging the readers to act in a certain way on a topic matter for the workplace.

Proposals have traditional sections that supply the information to the appropriate reader. A proposal will have a clear introduction, body, and conclusion. These sections will each have subsections to provide the detail that is necessary. Information that is included in a proposal is thoroughly researched and documented. Illustrations and graphics are used to clarify information and to direct the reader through the report.

Conventional Sections and Front and Back Matter of Formal Reports

Front Matter	Conventional Sections	Back (End) Matter
Letter of Transmittal	Introduction	Works Cited or List of
Cover	Methods	References
Title Page	Results	Glossary
Table of Contents	Conclusions	List of Abbreviations or
List of Illustrations	Recommendations	Symbols
Executive Summary		Appendices
(or Abstract)		Index

From *Technical Communication* by Brenda Sims. Copyright © 2015 by Kendall Hunt Publishing Company. Reprinted by permission.

TIPS for Writing the Letter of Transmittal

In the first paragraph . . .
- State the title or subject of the document.
- State the reason for preparing the document. For example, the reason might be to complete a class assignment, to respond to a request from a manager or client, or to complete a research project.

In the middle paragraph(s) . . .
- State the purpose of the document. (Some writers include the purpose in the first paragraph.)
- Summarize your conclusions and recommendations.
- *Optional:* Include and explain any changes to your work or the document since you last corresponded with the readers.

In the final paragraph . . .
- Offer to answer readers' questions about the document or its contents.
- *Optional:* Thank any person, group, or organization that helped you prepare the document.

Letter of Transmittal

Louisiana State University
Department of Biological Sciences
Choppin Hall
Baton Rouge, LA 70805

April 23, 2015

Dr. Louis Rowland
Director
Department of Wildlife and Fisheries
2000 Quail Drive
Baton Rouge, LA 70808
Re: Report on Black-Bellied Plover

Dear Dr. Rowland:

The first paragraph includes the title, the occasion, and the purpose of the document. →

I am pleased to submit the accompanying report, "Black-Bellied Plover Habitat in Louisiana," in response to your request. The report examines black-bellied plover habitat in Louisiana as part of a program to prevent this species from becoming endangered.

The second paragraph includes the conclusion, the recommendation, and information that especially interests the reader. →

For this report, I examined the literature about previous sightings of black-bellied plover in Louisiana and analyzed satellite images of those sighting locations. Based on this information, I have concluded that black-bellied plovers prefer pasture and shrub land. To protect the remaining black-bellied plover population, we must conserve and monitor the locations where the bird has been most frequently sighted.

In the third paragraph, the writer offers to answer questions. →

If you have any questions, please call me at (225) 555-1234 or email me at dbrown@verizon.net.

Sincerely,

Danielle Brown

Danielle Brown
Research Assistant

From *Technical Communication* by Brenda Sims. Copyright © 2015 by Kendall Hunt Publishing Company. Reprinted by permission.

Title Page from a Student Report

A title that indicates the subject and purpose of the document →

Black-Bellied Plover Habitat in Louisiana:
A Recommendation

Name of the intended readers →

Writer's name →

Writer's organization →

Date submitted →

Prepared for
Louisiana Department of Wildlife and Fisheries
By Danielle Brown
Louisiana State University
April 2015

Title Page from a Workplace Report

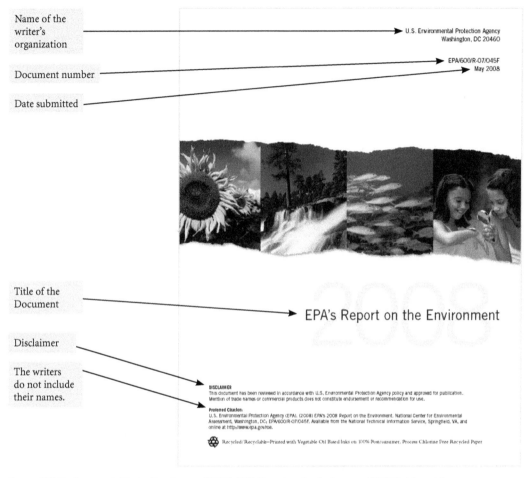

Name of the writer's organization → U.S. Environmental Protection Agency
Washington, DC 20460

Document number → EPA/600/R-07/045F

Date submitted → May 2008

Title of the Document → EPA's Report on the Environment

Disclaimer

The writers do not include their names.

DISCLAIMER
This document has been reviewed in accordance with U.S. Environmental Protection Agency policy and approved for publication. Mention of trade names or commercial products does not constitute endorsement or recommendation for use.

Preferred Citation:
U.S. Environmental Protection Agency (EPA). (2008) EPA's 2008 Report on the Environment. National Center for Environmental Assessment, Washington, DC; EPA/600/R-07/045F. Available from the National Technical Information Service, Springfield, VA, and online at http://www.epa.gov/roe.

Recycled/Recyclable—Printed with Vegetable Oil Based Inks on 100% Postconsumer, Process Chlorine Free Recycled Paper

Source: U.S. Environmental Protection Agency (2008). *EPA's Report on the Environment 2008.* Retrieved from http://cfpub.epa.gov/ncea/cfm/recordisplay.cfm?deid=190806.

From *Technical Communication* by Brenda Sims. Copyright © 2015 by Kendall Hunt Publishing Company. Reprinted by permission.

Uninformative Table of Contents

Contents

Acknowlegments i
Summary ii
List of Illustrations iii
Definition of the Problem 1
Background of the Problem 2
Methods 12
Results 29
Discussion 39
Conclusions and Recommendations 45
References 47
Appendixes 49

Effective Table of Contents

Right-align all
the numbers.

Show heading
levels by
indenting.

Vary the
type style to
indicate
heading levels.

Use the exact
wording that
appears in the
body of the
document.

Use guide dots.

Contents

Abstract . . . . **ii**

List of Illustrations . . . . **iv**

Introduction **1**

Black-Bellied Plover and Its Habitat **2**

    Description of Black-Bellied Plover **2**

    Habitat of Black-Bellied Plover **5**

    Migration of Black-Bellied Plover **7**

    Status of Black-Bellied Plover 11

Methods for Identifying Black-Bellied Plover Habitat **13**

    Historical Sightings of Black-Bellied Plover 14

    Satellite Imagery of the Habitat 20

        Rectifying the Images *23*

        Classifying the Landuse *27*

    Remote Sensing of the Habitat. 28

**Results from the Sightings Information, Satellite
Imagery, and Remote Sensing** **29**

    List of Historical Sightings of Black-Bellied Plover in
    Louisiana 30

    Landuse Classes in the Satellite Imagery. 32

    Landuse Class of Black-Bellied Plover Habitat 35

**Recommendation for Protecting Black-Bellied Plover
in Louisiana** **37**

    Landuse in the Black-Bellied Plover Habitat.. 38

    Habitat Areas in Louisiana 39

Works Cited **41**

Appendixes **42**

    A. Satellite Imagery of Similar Habitats along
      the Gulf Coast 43

    B. Remote Sensing of Similar Habitats along
      the Gulf Coast 49

Decimal-Style Table of Contents

"1" indicates the chapter or section—in this case, Chapter 1.

"3" indicates the third subsection of Chapter 1.

This number indicates the first subsection of Subsection 2 in Chapter 2.

Contents

Abstract ii
List of Illustrations iv
Introduction 1
1.0 Black-Bellied Plover and Its Habitat 2
    1.1 Description of Black-Bellied Plover 2
    1.2 Habitat of Black-Bellied Plover 5
    1.3 Migration of Black-Bellied Plover 7
    1.4 Status of Black-Bellied Plover....................... 11
2.0 Methods for Identifying Black-Bellied Plover Habitat... 13
    2.1 Historical Sightings of Black-Bellied Plover........... 14
    2.2 Satellite Imagery of the Habitat 20
        2.2 .1 *Rectifying the Images* 23
        2.2.2 *Classifying the Landuse* 27
    2.3 Remote Sensing of the Habitat...................... 28
3.0 Results from the Sightings Information, Satellite Imagery, and Remote Sensing 29
    3.1 List of Historical Sightings of Black-Bellied Plover in Louisiana 30
    3.2 Landuse Classes in the Satellite Imagery. 32
    3.3 Landuse Class of Black-Bellied Plover Habitat 35
4.0 Recommendation for Protecting Black-Bellied Plover in Louisiana 37
    4.1 Landuse in the Black-Bellied Plover Habitat.. 38
    4.2 Habitat Areas in Louisiana 39
Works Cited 41
Appendixes 42
    A. Satellite Imagery of Similar Habitats along the Gulf Coast 43
    B. Remote Sensing of Similar Habitats along the Gulf Coast................................... 49

Executive Summary Focusing on Conclusions and Recommendations

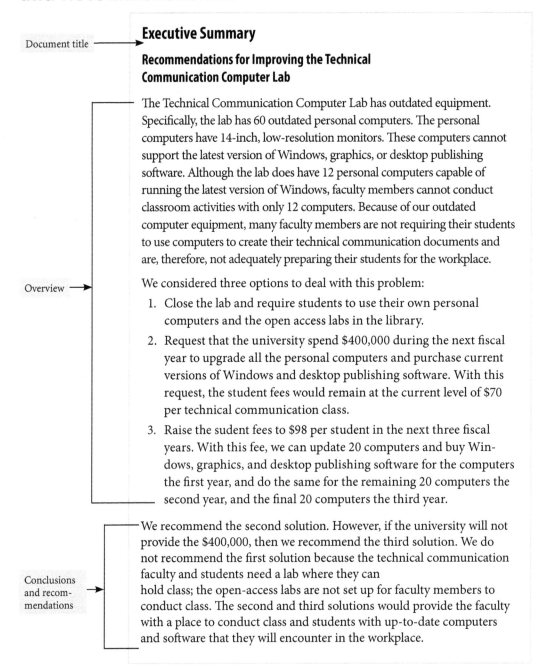

Document title

Executive Summary

Recommendations for Improving the Technical Communication Computer Lab

Overview

The Technical Communication Computer Lab has outdated equipment. Specifically, the lab has 60 outdated personal computers. The personal computers have 14-inch, low-resolution monitors. These computers cannot support the latest version of Windows, graphics, or desktop publishing software. Although the lab does have 12 personal computers capable of running the latest version of Windows, faculty members cannot conduct classroom activities with only 12 computers. Because of our outdated computer equipment, many faculty members are not requiring their students to use computers to create their technical communication documents and are, therefore, not adequately preparing their students for the workplace.

We considered three options to deal with this problem:

1. Close the lab and require students to use their own personal computers and the open access labs in the library.
2. Request that the university spend $400,000 during the next fiscal year to upgrade all the personal computers and purchase current versions of Windows and desktop publishing software. With this request, the student fees would remain at the current level of $70 per technical communication class.
3. Raise the sudent fees to $98 per student in the next three fiscal years. With this fee, we can update 20 computers and buy Windows, graphics, and desktop publishing software for the computers the first year, and do the same for the remaining 20 computers the second year, and the final 20 computers the third year.

Conclusions and recommendations

We recommend the second solution. However, if the university will not provide the $400,000, then we recommend the third solution. We do not recommend the first solution because the technical communication faculty and students need a lab where they can hold class; the open-access labs are not set up for faculty members to conduct class. The second and third solutions would provide the faculty with a place to conduct class and students with up-to-date computers and software that they will encounter in the workplace.

Page Numbering of a Formal Document

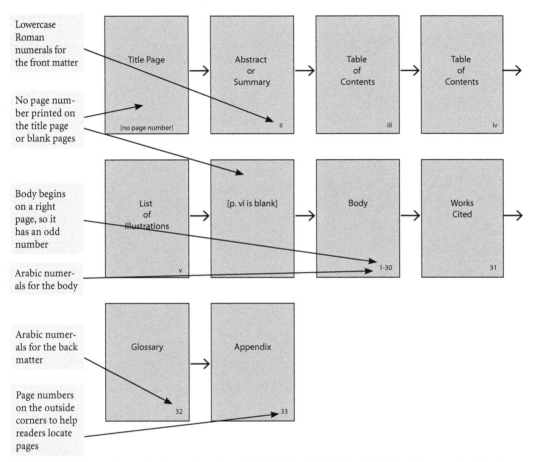

Lowercase Roman numerals for the front matter

No page number printed on the title page or blank pages

Body begins on a right page, so it has an odd number

Arabic numerals for the body

Arabic numerals for the back matter

Page numbers on the outside corners to help readers locate pages

Title Page
[no page number]

Abstract or Summary
ii

Table of Contents
iii

Table of Contents
iv

List of Illustrations
v

[p. vi is blank]

Body
1-30

Works Cited
31

Glossary
32

Appendix
33

From *Technical Communication* by Brenda Sims. Copyright © 2015 by Kendall Hunt Publishing Company. Reprinted by permission.

CHAPTER 10

Recommendations

Table Used to Rank Options Based on Criteria (5 Is the Highest Rating)

Option	Cost	Processor Speed	Display Size (larger is preferred)	Weight (lighter is preferred)	Hard Drive Size	Total Points
Micro Express IFL9025	5	4	3	4	4	20
Lenovo ThinkPad T61p	2	4	3	5	1	15
HP Pavilion HDX	1	3	5	1	5	15
Dell Inspiron 1720	3	3	4	2	4	16
Apple Macbook Pro	4	5	4	4	3	20

From *Technical Communication* by Brenda Sims. Copyright © 2015 by Kendall Hunt Publishing Company. Reprinted by permission.

Using Criteria Other Than Cost to Evaluate Two Closely Ranked Options

Option	Processor Speed	Display Size (larger is preferred)	Weight (lighter is preferred)	Hard Drive Size	Total Points
Micro Express IFL9025	4	3	4	4	15
Apple Macbook Pro	5	4	4	3	16

From *Technical Communication* by Brenda Sims. Copyright © 2015 by Kendall Hunt Publishing Company. Reprinted by permission.

Comparing by Criteria in the Results Section

Cost of Laptop (*criterion*)
- Micro Express (option)
- Lenovo ThinkPad
- HP Pavilion
- Dell Inspiron
- Apple Macbook Pro

Processor Speed (*criterion*)
- Micro Express
- Lenovo ThinkPad
- HP Pavilion
- Dell Inspiron
- Apple Macbook Pro

Display Size (*criterion*)
- Micro Express
- Lenovo ThinkPad
- HP Pavilion
- Dell Inspiron
- Apple Macbook Pro

Weight (*criterion*)
- Micro Express
- Lenovo ThinkPad
- HP Pavilion
- Dell Inspiron
- Apple Macbook Pro

Hard Drive Size (*criterion*)
- Micro Express
- Lenovo ThinkPad
- HP Pavilion
- Dell Inspiron
- Apple Macbook Pro

From *Technical Communication* by Brenda Sims. Copyright © 2015 by Kendall Hunt Publishing Company. Reprinted by permission.

Comparing by Options in the Results Section

Micro Express (*option*)
- Cost of the laptop (criterion)
- Processor speed
- Display size
- Weight
- Hard drive size

Lenovo ThinkPad (*option*)
- Cost of the laptop
- Processor speed
- Display size
- Weight
- Hard drive size

HP Pavilion (*option*)
- Cost of the laptop
- Processor speed
- Display size
- Weight
- Hard drive size

Dell Inspiron (*option*)
- Cost of the laptop
- Processor speed
- Display size
- Weight
- Hard drive size

Apple Macbook Pro (*option*)
- Cost of the laptop
- Processor speed
- Display size
- Weight
- Hard drive size

From *Technical Communication* by Brenda Sims. Copyright © 2015 by Kendall Hunt Publishing Company. Reprinted by permission.

Recommendation Report (General Example)

General Concepts and Practices for the Creation of an Informal Recommendation Report

Introduction

This portion of the work should establish a clear purpose for the report with consideration to your selected audience. It should briefly discuss the intended function of the overall work in summation saving the detail for later in the report, but ensuring a clear and certain goal and scope. By the end of this section, the audience to whom you are writing should understand why they are reading this, what it aims to accomplish, and an overview of how to go about doing so. The following subsections of the recommendation report will provide all of the necessary information to fully answer your audience's questions. However, this Introduction portion should not build intrigue or leave any uncertainties; while it should capture the audience's attention, it should not be vague or unclear in any regards.

Subtitle Pertaining to General Information

Begin with the basic information, here more detailed than in your Introduction, pertaining to your purpose. In essence, this section should be about the "*what*" regarding your subject matter. Explain any basic information the reader(s) may require or that you wish to review here. This section should lay the groundwork to ensure that your audience understands the current situation regarding the topic(s) discussed here. You may highlight key information in this section by using bulleted key words or phrases, such as:

- Any facts or figures required
- Specific Numbers or information
- Details or concerns you wish to itemize

Subtitle Discussing Background Information

As the report continues, further detailed information should be provided to elaborate on why the audience should agree with your proposed recommendation. Think of this as the "*why*" section of the report. Be sure to highlight how agreeing to your purpose would benefit the audience. Don't talk about why you want to do this: focus on what their needs, wants, and/or concerns would be in this area. Preemptively answer their questions of "*why should we do this?*" or "*what's in this for me?*" before proceeding to how this could be done. Consider their concerns, such as:

- Why this should/should not be done
- Explain your timeframe, or any urgency to this situation
- How doing this would benefit your audience, or not doing so would be a detriment
- What impact this would have on the audience, or something concerning to them

Subtitle Regarding Methods or Procedures Involved

Once your audience understands and appreciates why your purpose is relevant and important, you should then discuss what you recommend be done. Consider this the "*how*" portion of the work, discussing what specifically would occur. Fully explain the details of how to implement your recommended purpose. Be sure the audience can understand the steps or concepts involved in doing what you recommend they do. Once again, preemptively answer the questions your reader(s) may pose. You may need to detail:

1. How this begins
2. What would then follow
3. How to then proceed
4. What will come next in the process

Recommendation Report (General Example) *continued*

5. All necessary steps, however many there may be, to complete this process
6. The final step required

Once your audience understands the implementation of your recommendation overall, you may then need to provide further detail to expand upon or substantiate your ideas.

Subtitle on Data or Further Information

One or more sections here may offer information to further develop, substantiate, or expand upon your topic. Expand upon the "how" and "why" you have discussed. This may likely include:

Tables I: Various Tables

Relevant Data	A	B
1	XXXX	XXXXX XXXXXXX XXXXX
2	XXXXX	XXXXXXX XXXX XXXXXXXX
3	XXX	XXXX XXXXX XXXXXXX
4	XXXXX	XX XXXXX XXXXXXX

Tables II: Various Tables

Required Info	i	ii	iii
I	X.X	X.X	X.X
II	X.X	X.X	X.X
III	X.X	X.X	X.X
IV	X.X	X.X	X.X

Subtitle on Data or Further Information

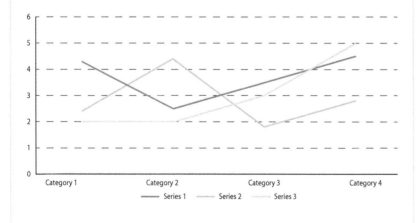

Recommendation Report (General Example) *continued*

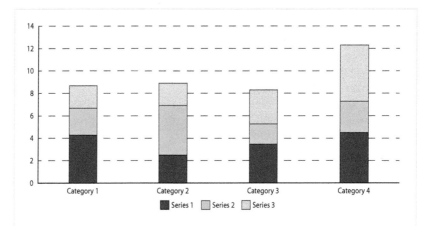

Conclusion

This is a summation of the preceding information provided throughout the report, meant to tie it all together. It should provide closure or completion for your audience regarding your purpose. Detail the conclusions you have drawn in terms of how they apply to your reader(s). Consider this a 'wrap-up', or final thoughts regarding the topic. Be sure to discuss any results, observed or anticipated, that you wish to include. Don't simply repeat what you've already said; rather, provide a closing to it.

Recommendation

To put it simply, here you discuss what should come next following your report. Moving forward, what do you recommend? This may pertain to you, the audience, or any other involved parties. Your recommendations may include:

- Future studies to be conducted
- More information that may need to be gathered to continue
- What steps should be taken next
- What you will do following this report
- What your audience can or should do next
- What changes should be implemented moving forward
- Who will next be involved in this process

Recommendation Report

Because the readers are biologists, the writers use technical terminology the readers will understand and expect.

Biotic Characterization of Small Streams in the Vicinity of Oil Retention Ponds 1 and 2 Near the Y-12 Plant

Introduction

This report provides data on the aquatic biota in the streams near the oil retention ponds west of the Y-12 place at Oak Ridge National Laboratory. Built in 1943, the Y-12 plant originally produced nuclear weapon components and subassemblies and supported the Department of Energy's weapon-design laboratories. In the production of the subassemblies, the plant used materials such as enriched uranium, lithium hydride, and deteride. The plant disposed of both solid and liquid wastes in burial facilities in Bear Creek Vally—approximately one mile west of the plant site. This report fulfills the Department of Energy's commitment to assess the aquatic biota near the man-made oil retention pond in the valley.

Methods

The writers list the specific sites studied.

The Environmental Sciences Division conducted quantitative sampling of benthic macroinvertebrates and fish at the following sites:

- Bear Creek above and below the confluence with Stream A, a small tributary that drains Oil Retention Pond 1 (Stations 1 and 2, respectively)
- Stream 1A just above the confluence with Bear Creek (Station 3)
- Stream 2, a small uncontaminated tributary of Bear Creek that flows adjacent to Bear Creek Road (Station 4, the control station)

We also conducted qualitative sampling at the following sites in the watersheds of Oil Retention Ponds 1 and 2:
Stream 1A, immediately below Pond 1 (Station 5)

- The diversion ditch that carries surface runoff from portions of Burial Grounds B, C, D, and the area north of Burial Ground A to Stream 1A just below the pond (Station 6)
- Stream 1A above the diversion ditch (Station 7)
- Oil Retention Pond 2 (Station 8)
- We could not sample above or below Pond 2 because of insufficient flows. We did not sample Oil Retention Pond 1.

The writers use lists and subheads to identify the methods for sampling benthic macroinvertebrates and fishes.

Methods for Sampling Benthic Macroinvertebrates

To sample the benthic macroinvertebrates at Stations 1B-4B (three samples per site), we followed these procedures:

1. Placed a 27 x 33 cm metal frame on the bottom of the stream in the riffle area.
2. Held a 363-m mesh drift net at the downstream end of the metal frame while agitating the stream bottom (within the frame) with a metal rod. The stream flow transported suspended materials into the net.
3. Washed the net three times with the stream water to concentrate the sample and remove fine sediments.
4. Transferred the sample to glass jars that contained approximately 10% formalin to preserve the sample.

In the laboratory, we followed these procedures to analyze the samples:

1. Washed each sample using a standard No. 35 mesh (500 m) sieve and placed the washed sample in a large white tray.

Recommendation Report *continued*

> The writers use specific, detailed language so that readers can duplicate their methods. This language also helps to justify their conclusions and recommendations.

2. Examined large pieces of debris (e.g., leaves and twigs) for organisms and then removed the debris not containing organisms.
3. Covered the contents of the tray with a saturated sucrose solution and agitated the tray to separate the organisms from the debris.
4. Identified all organisms that floated to the surface by taxonomic order or family.
5. Collectively weighed (to the nearest 0.1 g) the individuals in each taxonomic group.

Methods for Sampling Fishes

We used a Smith-Root Type XV backpack electro shocker to sample the fish community at Stations 1F-3F. This electroshocker can deliver up to 1200 V of pulsed direct current. We used a pulse frequency of 120 Hz at all times and adjusted the output voltage to the optimal value, based on the water conductivity at the site. We measured the conductivity with a Hydrolab Digital 4041. This instrument also concurrently measured the water temperature and pH.

At each of the sampling stations, we followed these methods to sample the fish community:

1. Made a single pass upstream and downstream using a representative reach. The length of the reach varied among sites (from 22 to 115 m).
2. Held captured fish in a 0.64-cm plastic-mesh cage until we completed the sampling.
3. Anesthetized the fish in the field with MS-222 (tricane methane sulfonate).
4. Counted the fish by species and collectively weighed the individuals of a given species to the nearest 0.5 g on a triple-beam balance.
5. Released the fish to the stream.

In a preliminary sampling we collected representative individuals of each species by seining and preserved the fish in 10% formalin. In the laboratory, we identified the fish using these methods:

1. Identified species using unpublished taxonomic keys of Etnier (1976).
2. Compared the mountain redbelly dace (Phoxinus Oreas) and the common shiner (Notropis Cornutus) with specimens collected from Ish Creek, a small stream on the south slope of West Chestnut Ridge, and identified as Phoxinus Oreas and Notropis Cornutus.

Results

> The writers use parenthetical notes to refer readers to tables.

This section presents results of the sampling and analyzing of the benthic macroinvertebrates and of the fishes in the study sites.

Benthic Macroinvertebrates

Qualitative sampling at the sites near Oil Retention Pond 1 and in Pond 2 resulted in few samples (see Table I). We also found low densities in the quantitative samples taken from Stream lA, which drains Oil Retention Pond 1, and in Bear Creek near the confluence with Stream lA (see Tables II and III). Relatively high densities and biomass of benthic organisms appeared in Stream 2, a small uncontaminated tributary of Bear Creek (Station 4). Some of the differences in the composition of the benthic community between this site and others may have occurred because of sub-strate differences (e.g., the large amounts of detritus in Stream 2 when compared to the predominately small rubble and gravel at Stations 1 and 2). However, a depauperate benthic fauna existed in Bear Creek and Stream lA.

Recommendation Report *continued*

3

Table I. Description of qualitative sampling conducted near oil Retention Ponds 1 and 2 west of the Y-12 Plant (previous study)

The writers summarize results in tables.

Station	Location	Method	Sampling Results
5	Stream 1A just below Oil Retention Pond 1	Kick-seining	No organisms found
6	Diversion ditch just west of Oil Retention Pond 1	Kick-seining	No organisms found
7	Stream lA above the diversion ditch	Kick-seining	Few Isopoda; unidentified salamander
8	Oil Retention Pond 2	Dip-netting; removal of sediment/litter from margins of ponds	No organisms found

The writers use graphics to present the results.

Table II. Total number and weight (g, in parentheses) of benthic macroinvertebrates in each of three 27×33 cm bottom samples collected from four sampling sites in the vicinity of Y-12 Oil Retention Pond 1

	Sampling Station			
Sample no.	1B	2B	3B	4B
1	0	0	0	53 (0.8)
2	0	2 (0.1)	3 (0.1)	46 (2.2)
3	0	2 (0.1)	0	25 (1.0)
Mean no./m^2 (g/m^2)	0	14.9 (7.1)	11.2 (0.4)	501.3 (15.3)
Substrate	Coarse gravel embedded in sand and silt; leaf packs uncommon	Same as Station 1B	Sand, silt, mud, and detritus/ leaves	Deep soft mud covered by leaves and woody debris

Recommendation Report *continued*

4

Table III. Density (mean no./m²) of various benthic macroinvertebrate taxa in bottom samples collected from four sampling sites in the vicinity of Y-12 Oil Retention Pond 1. Biomass (wet weight, g/m²) in parentheses. NC=None Collected.

Taxon	Sampling Station			
	1B	2B	3B[a]	4B
Amphipoda	NC	NC	NC	67.3(0.6)
Annelida	NC	7.5(0.4)	NC	NC
Chironomidae	NC	NC	NC	273.1(0.7)
Decapoda	NC	NC	NC	22.4(7.1)
Isopoda	NC	NC	NC	86.1(1.9)
Oligochaeta	NC	NC	11.2(0.4)	NC
Sialidae	NC	3.7(1.5)	NC	NC
Tipulidae	NC	3.7(5.2)	NC	7.5(3.7)
Tricoptera	NC	NC	NC	44.9(1.3)

[a]Damselfly nymph collected by kick-seining.

Fishes

The four fish species collected at the four sample sites commonly inhabit small streams on the Department of Energy Oak Ridge Reservation. For example, these four species were the most abundant fishes found by electrofishing in Ish Creek, a small, undisturbed tributary of the Clinch River that drains the south slope of Chestnut Ridge. The presence of fish in the lower reaches of Stream 1A is consistent with the results of a bioassay conducted on the water from Oil Retention Pond 1. This bioassay showed no mortality to bluegill sunfish after 96 hours (Giddings). The high density and biomass of fish at Station 3F may relate to the abundant periphyton growth observed in the winter and to the chemistry of the effluent from Oil Retention Pond 1.

We found no aquatic species listed as threatened or endangered by either the U.S. Fish and Wildlife Service or the State of Tennessee. However, the Tennessee Wildlife Resources Agency has identified the mountain redbelly dace (Phoxinus Oreas) as a species which, though not considered threatened within the state, may not currently exist at or near their optimum carrying capacity (see Table IV).

Recommendation Report *continued*

5

Table IV. Density (mean no./m^2) of various benthic macroinvertebrate taxa in bottom samples collected from four sampling sites in the vicinity of Y-12 Oil Retention Pond 1. Biomass (wet weight, g/m^2) in parentheses. NC=None Collected.

Species	Sampling Station		
	1F	2F	3F
Blacknose dace (*Rynichthys atratulus*)	8(21.0)	1(1.5)	2(2.5)
Common shiner (*Notropis cornutus*)	3(22.5)	0	1(6.5)
Creek chub (*Semotilus atromaculatus*)	42(204.5)	4(76.5)	10(64.0)
Mountain redbelly dace (*Phoxinus oreas*)	39(64.0)	1 (3.5)	35(51.0)
Total (*all species combined*)			
Density (no./m^2)	0.30	0.03	1.68
Biomass (g/m^2)	1.00	0.41	4.33
Physical characteristics of sampling site			
Length of stream sampled (m)	115	91	22
Mean width (m)	2.7	2.2	1.3
Mean depth (m)	19	13	10
Conductivity (S/cm)	260	1005	477
Water temperature (*C)	8.5	0.5	1.5
pH	7.1	7.6	7.5

Recommendation Report *continued*

The writers interpret the results. → **Conclusions**

The Y-12 Plan operations have had an adverse impact on the benthic communities of Bear Creek and some of its tributaries. The low benthic densities at Station 2B just above the confluence with Stream lA suggest that the source of impact is not limited to the effluent from Oil Retention Pond 1. The relatively low fish density at Station 2F also implies an upstream perturbation (such as the S-3 ponds).

Further evidence of upstream impact(s) is available from the results of a similar study conducted 10 years prior to this study. In this study, researchers sampled benthic macroinvertebrates and fish at two sites located 50 m about and 100 m below the Y-12 sanitary landfill site. The west end of the landfill is approximately 1.4 stream kilometers about the confluence of Stream 1A with Bear Creek. No benthic organisms or fish were collected at either of the two sites, and in situ fish bioassays conducted just about and 500 m below the landfill resulted in 100% mortality after 24 hours.

The results of the earlier study differ significantly from those of the present study. The current presence of fish at Station 2F, which is approximately 500 m below the site of the earlier bioassays, may indicate changes in water quality over the past 10 years. However, the occurrence of fish in this region of Bear Creek may only be a temporary phenomenon. In view of the information currently available, both explanations of the difference in results seem equally plausible.

The writers present only the recommendations here. → **Recommendations**

We recommend additional studies to address several important issues:

- More extensive season sampling of the benthic macroinvertebrate and fish communit'ies to obtain a complete inventory of the aquatic biota in Bear Creek watershed, to investigate the potential recovery of biotic communities downstream of the confluence of Stream 1A, and to identify specific sources of impact to aquatic biota in Bear Creek about the confluence with Stream1A.
- In situ and acute bioassays to assist with identifying potential sources of impact.
- Chronic bioassays to determine the effects on biota of long-term exposure to effluent sources.
- Studies of storms and their role in transporting contaminants downstream and in establishing and/or recovering the biotic communities in Bear Creek.

Source: Adapted from Loar, J. M. and D. K. Cox, *Biotic Characterization of Small Streams in the Vicinity of Oil Retention Ponds 1 and 2 Near the Y-12 Plant Bear Creek Valley Waste Disposal Area.* Jan. 31, 1984. Oak Ridge National Laboratory, Oak Ridge, TN.

CHAPTER 11

Writing for the Web

TIPS for Making Text Easy to Read and Scan

- **Write in small chunks** (Bradbury, 2000; Spyridakis, 2000). Small chunks help users scan pages. Break long paragraphs and pages into shorter ones. Put less information on each page, and use only one idea in each paragraph (Bradbury, 2000; Nielsen, 1997b). By chunking the information, you help users more easily locate information and retain it.
- **Group related information.** Use the principle of proximity to group related information (see Chapter 10). The excerpt from a Web page in Figure 19.1 effectively groups related information, so users can scan the page and locate the information they need. For example, if users are interested in science in national parks, they can find that information by simply scanning the headings.
- **Use bulleted items and lists when appropriate.** (Bradbury, 2000; Nielsen, 1997b). Bulleted items and lists visually break up text, make pages easier to read, and guide users to information.
- **Use subheadings.** Subheadings categorize information and help users scan the page.
- **Use a consistent design for the pages.** The pages should look like they belong to the same website or online document, so select an appropriate color scheme and use it consistently throughout. For example, use the same color for the same elements and the same background color for every page. The Web pages in Figure 19.2 have a consistent page design: the navigation bar and the company logo are in the same place on both pages and the pages use the same colors.
- **Use ample white space.** Create contrast by including ample white space (or blank space). If a page is filled with text and/or graphics, users may not want to read the page or may not know what information is important. User-focused websites and online documents use white space to highlight and organize information. Don't be tempted to fill up the page just because you can.
- **Use simple words and short sentences.** Eliminate unnecessary detail and use as few words as possible.
- **Include an introduction or introductory sentence that identifies the purpose of the website and specifies the intended users.** On the homepage, introduce the purpose of the website. If you're writing for an organization, introduce the organization and possibly link to a page that gives information about that organization. This page might be called "About Us."

Effectively Grouped Information on a Web Page

Source: http://www.nature.nps.gov/

From *Technical Communication* by Brenda Sims. Copyright © 2015 by Kendall Hunt Publishing Company. Reprinted by permission.

Consistent Web Page Layout

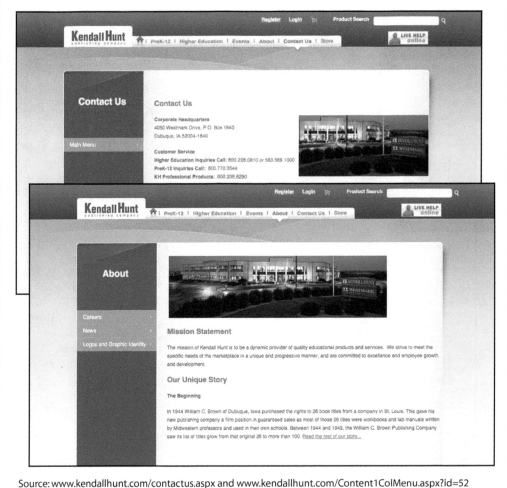

Source: www.kendallhunt.com/contactus.aspx and www.kendallhunt.com/Content1ColMenu.aspx?id=52

From *Technical Communication* by Brenda Sims. Copyright © 2015 by Kendall Hunt Publishing Company. Reprinted by permission.

Site Map

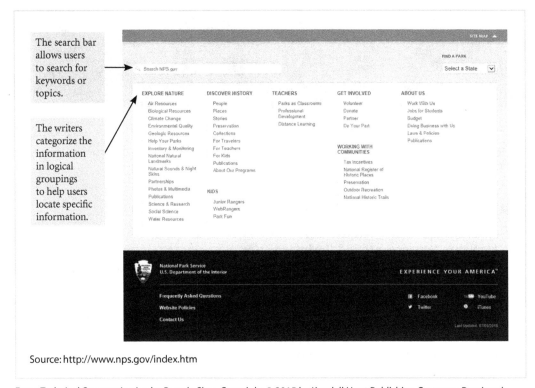

The search bar allows users to search for keywords or topics.

The writers categorize the information in logical groupings to help users locate specific information.

Source: http://www.nps.gov/index.htm

From *Technical Communication* by Brenda Sims. Copyright © 2015 by Kendall Hunt Publishing Company. Reprinted by permission.

Header on a Website

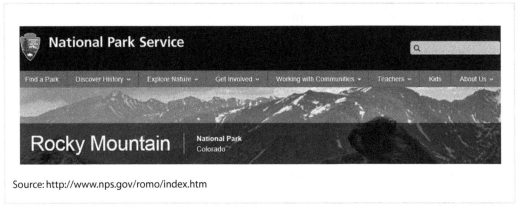

Source: http://www.nps.gov/romo/index.htm

From *Technical Communication* by Brenda Sims. Copyright © 2015 by Kendall Hunt Publishing Company. Reprinted by permission.

Footer on a Website

Source: http://www.nps.gov/romo/index.htm

TIPS for Creating Clear Links[1]

- **Structure sentences around the information you want to reinforce.** Don't structure the sentence around the link. Focus on the information, not the link as in the following examples. The first example is awkward while the second example is easy to read:
  - *Focuses on the link*   **Click here** for more information on the national register of historic places.
  - *Focuses on the*   The **National Register of Historic Places** page links to a list
  - *information*   of historic places authorized by the National Historic Preservation Act.
- **Make the link informative.** Provide the users with an informative description of the page that will load. Users want to know what information will appear when they click on the link. If the link is not descriptive, the user may waste time chasing minor or undesired information.
  - *Not descriptive*   **Click here for more information** on handwashing.
  - *Descriptive*   Follow **proper handwashing procedures** established by the New York Department of Health to ensure that you don't spread germs.
- **Use underlining and conventional colors for links.** Links are traditionally underlined blue text. While underlining can make some letterforms unreadable, you should use it for links embedded in text. The underlining ensures that users can identify a link with or without color. Unless you have a justifiable reason to change the blue to another color, use blue for embedded links.

[1] Adapted from Lynch & Horton (2011).

Excerpt from a Home Page

The header clearly identifies the page as belonging to the National Park Service.

The page is credible because it uses high-quality, relevant photos.

The page includes two search engines: one allows users to search by keywords and another allows users to locate a park by state.

The page is easy to navigate. It includes a horizontal navigation bar with clear contrast to help users locate the pages of the website.

The information is effectively chunked with subheadings.

The footer helps users to connect with others through social media. The footer also makes the site credible and reliable because it includes the date last updated and the website policies.

The page engages the users through social media by inviting them to share their stories related to National Parks.

Source: http://www.nps.gov/index.htm

From *Technical Communication* by Brenda Sims. Copyright © 2015 by Kendall Hunt Publishing Company. Reprinted by permission.

Excerpt from an "About Us" Page

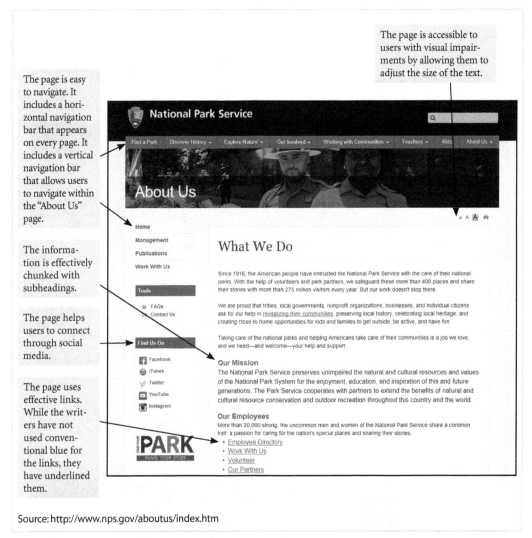

The page is accessible to users with visual impairments by allowing them to adjust the size of the text.

The page is easy to navigate. It includes a horizontal navigation bar that appears on every page. It includes a vertical navigation bar that allows users to navigate within the "About Us" page.

The information is effectively chunked with subheadings.

The page helps users to connect through social media.

The page uses effective links. While the writers have not used conventional blue for the links, they have underlined them.

Source: http://www.nps.gov/aboutus/index.htm

From *Technical Communication* by Brenda Sims. Copyright © 2015 by Kendall Hunt Publishing Company. Reprinted by permission.

Ethics Note

Copyright, Intellectual Property, and the Web

Have you ever found a graphic that you liked on a website and used it on your personal website? Have you copied code from a website and used it for your organization's site? Have you ever used a company's logo or trademark from a website? If so, you could be guilty of copyright, patent, or trademark infringement. U.S. and international laws protect every element of a website: the text, graphics, and the code (Le Vie, 2000). Even if the authors of a site haven't filed a formal copyright application, the law protects their work. Along with copyrights, the law protects an organization's patents, trademarks, and trade secrets. You or your organization can "bruise its reputation by infringing on someone else's copyright" or intellectual property; and you could face legal penalties for it (Le Vie, 2000, p. 21).

You must protect your website, your intellectual property, and your organization's products and services. For example, aspirin originally started as a trademarked product, but the manufacturer failed to protect its trademark; and aspirin became a name used by many manufacturers. To protect your website and your intellectual property—or that of your organization—follow these guidelines to maintain the uniqueness of your product or service:

- Place a copyright notice in the footer of every page, not just on the homepage.
- Link from the word "copyright" to another Web page that defines what you own on the site (Le Vie, 2000) .

Protect yourself and your company from the legal penalties and bruised reputations that occur when you don't respect the copyrights and intellectual property of others:

- Obtain permission for any information, graphic, or code that you use from another site or printed document.
- Place the permission, copyright, and trademark information in a conspicuous place.
- *Do not use any information, graphic, or code without the written permission of its authors.*

From *Technical Communication* by Brenda Sims. Copyright © 2015 by Kendall Hunt Publishing Company. Reprinted by permission.

Exercises

1. Locate two websites on the same topic: one should be credible and trustworthy; one should be less credible and untrustworthy.
   a. Write a memo to your instructor comparing and contrasting the two sites. Include specific examples from the sites. (For help with the comparison and contrast pattern of organization, see Chapter 6).
   b. In your memo, include the URL for each Web page.

2. Locate the website for a national or local nonprofit organization such as the Red Cross or the American Heart Association. Analyze the following aspects of the site:
   - consistency of the page design
   - color (see Chapter 11 to review the information on color)
   - ease of navigation
   - style of writing
   - appropriateness of content

   Write an informal report to your instructor analyzing problems with the site and recommending solutions. Print a copy of the organization's homepage to attach to your report. (See Chapter 6 to review the problem and solution pattern of organization and Chapter 14 for information on reports.)

3. Evaluate the website of your hometown and compare it to the sites of two cities of similar size. As part of your evaluation, consider whether the site has the characteristics of a user-focused website:
   - Is it easy to scan?
   - Does it use concise language?
   - Is it easy to navigate?
   - Is it accessible?
   - Is it credible and trustworthy?

   Write a letter to the mayor or city manager summarizing your evaluation and comparisons. Turn in a copy of your letter to your instructor.

4. Expand your evaluation of your hometown's website. Determine
   - if the site has appropriately protected its copyright and other intellectual property, such as its logo (its branding).
   - if the site may have infringed on the copyrighted information or trademarks of others.

   Based on your evaluation, write a memo to your instructor explaining what you were looking for and whether the site adequately protects the city's intellectual property and branding and properly uses copyrighted information.

CPSIA information can be obtained
at www.ICGtesting.com
Printed in the USA
LVHW020900220819
628459LV00001B/1/P